T

Comments From Tim's Blog Postings

"Amen Tim, great post" - *Julie M.*

"Eloquently written" - *Laura*

"Thank you for articulating so well what I have felt for a long time." - *VivaHist*

"Quit making so much sense. You're making the U.S. Government look stupid." - *Capt. Karl*

"You have put so eloquently and candidly everything I agree with in writing a truly work of art." - *Sek Cheong*

"I love this guy" - *Vicki*

"I don't know why, but I love this guy" - *Diane*

"Amazing." - *Jonathon*

"Brilliant and directly to the heart of the matter." - *Robert*

"Some of the best commentary on the internet." - *Tom*

"One of the best 4th of July posts I have ever read." - *Chris*

"Elegant" - *Milner*

"I bet you eat poor people! You suck!" - *anonymous*

"Thank you for your interest in our campaign. And for the record, I do not eat poor people." - *Dr. Tim*

Acknowledgments

I am grateful for:

My wife Joanne - if we are honest about it, men achieve to impress the girls. If we are lucky, we get to spend our whole life trying to impress just one. I am very lucky.

My late father, Kenneth, my son Erik, and my brother Dave, each for obvious reasons.

Linda Werth, who brings Moment Of Clarity to the world each week and without whom there would be neither blog nor book.

Wayne C. Oldenburg, for allowing me to discover how high is up for me and encouraging me to try.

Ayn Rand, Milton Friedman, and Og Mandino. Hundreds of authors have influenced me; three have changed me.

Author's Introduction

I didn't set out to write a book.

After the 2008 elections, I decided to run for the U.S. House of Representatives from Wisconsin's 2nd District as a Libertarian Party candidate in 2010. The Democrat incumbent was, and is, ultra-liberal Tammy Baldwin.

So I started writing a weekly blog to introduce my campaign to the voters and to distinguish Libertarians from the two establishment parties. Later, when I withdrew from the race due to relocation, I changed its name from *Tim, Not Tammy*, to *Dr. Tim's Moment Of Clarity* and kept on writing.

With prose like "we are the party of hell no!" and "I want to be your Congressman, not your Mommy", our campaign got noticed the burgeoning Tea Party movement and by Liberty advocates across the nation.

Now *Dr. Tim's Moment Of Clarity* is carried on dozens of websites, shared across all of the social networks, and featured on numerous e-newsletters; its reach is measured in the hundreds of thousands.

Tooth Fairy Government is a collection of blog posts selected from the archives of *Dr. Tim's Moment Of Clarity* - articles, op-eds, campaign speeches, and letters to newspaper editors written between November 2008 and July 2010, both during and after the campaign. They appear here is no particular order.

It's all here somewhere: Libertarian philosophy, socialism, capitalism, Obama, health care, taxes, national security, economics, foreign policy, drugs, education energy, race, sound money, Democrats and Republicans, tea parties, climate change, immigration, guns, and of course, Tammy.

I write to make to make Libertarian ideas accessible to a broad audience, to make our principles relevant. Liberty is the absence of government in choice; it is not so complicated.

Thank you for reading my book. I hope you enjoy it.

Tim Nerenz, Ph.D.

TABLE OF CONTENTS

Tooth Fairy Government 11

Free Markets 13

Dr. Tim's Campaign Stump Speech 16

None of Your Business.. 18

Liberty Is... 20

FLIP... 23

You Might Be A Libertarian 25

The Real Minimum Wage Is Zero 28

What Comes After Stupid?.. 29

Defending The American Dream 31

Corporatista! 33

Voluntary Exchange.. 36

Constitution of Convenience 38

A Fair Tax 40

A Sensible Foreign Policy.. 42

A Strong Defense.. 44

A Woman's Right To Choose 47

Abolish The What?.. 50

Affirmative Action 53

Afghanistan 55

- Age of Consent Is 18 57
- Ba-Roke Obama 59
- BTU Bucks 61
- California Dreamin' 63
- Channeling Enron 66
- Chump Change 69
- Climatista! 72
- RepubliCoke And DemoPepsi 74
- Crap and Tirade 76
- More Cap and Less Trade 78
- Dangerous Weapons 81
- Energy Choice 85
- EU – Say It Like It Is Written 88
- Don't Stop At Health Care 90
- Fairtax 92
- Foreign Policy 94
- Get Your Shovels Ready 97
- Government We Don't Need 100
- Grow Up 103
- Hate Speech 104
- Heads And Tails 107
- Health Care Town Hall Speech 109

Individualism 111

Identity Theft Alert.. 113

Who Pays?.. 115

Immigration Reform 117

In Exchange For What 120

Independence Day.. 123

Irreconcilable Differences 127

Keeping Us Honest 129

Killing Our Golden Geese 131

Rights, Laws, and Victimless Crimes.................................. 133

Lessons Learned and Re-learned 136

Let It Snow... 138

Libertarian Party of Wisconsin 2010 Convention Speech 140

Libertarian Party of Wisconsin 2009 Convention Speech 144

Marx, Robin Hood, and Obama 148

Math Reform.. 151

Medical Choice... 154

Medical Choice – Part II 157

Misplaced Outrage 160

Missing The Point 163

Congress Votes On Mob Rule 164

Money and Taxes 167

Money For Nothing	170
National Security	173
No Cap, Free Trade	176
No Means No	178
Rookie	180
One In A Row	182
Other People's Money	184
Poor People	187
Public Option Airways	190
Public Transportation	193
Quit Talking Stupid	196
Real Health Care Reform	199
Represent, Not Rule	202
Republican Women of the North – Health Care Forum	204
Rights and Entitlements	208
Rights For Seniors	210
Your Right to Health Care	212
The Problem with Government	214
Pool Boy	217
Arrested Development	219
Independence Revisited	221
Counting Snouts	224

Smart People 227

Curing Cancer 230

Card Check Cannibals 232

Jobs 235

Thou Shall Not Steal 237

The 100 Yard Dash 240

Compassion 243

Equality 246

TOOTH FAIRY GOVERNMENT

Tim Nerenz, Ph.D.

Copyright © 2010 Timothy T. Nerenz
All rights reserved.

No part of this work may be reproduced without written permission

Tooth Fairy Government

I call it Tooth Fairy Government: they steal *your* quarter, put it under *their* kid's pillow, and make believe we are 25 cents richer.

If you are the child on the receiving end, you like Tooth Fairy Government.

It promises to buy your car, pay your mortgage, send you to college, pay for your health care, create a green job for you, pay your pension, and bailout your business if you fail.

And Tooth Fairy Government promises to do all that without raising your taxes, increasing your debt, burning a single gram of carbon, costing a single job, creating a single percentage point of inflation, or leaving a single child behind.

Your end of the bargain is to remain a child; an irresponsible, selfish, demanding, jealous child, focused solely on your own needs and desires, and totally oblivious to the rights of others.

You must believe you are entitled to that quarter, and you must accept that you are incapable of earning it for yourself.

You must learn to hate the child who was deprived when it was stolen from his parents, and you must agree to blame *them* for your troubles.

You must call the theft of their quarters "justice", and describe your perpetual dependence as "the public good".

That is the only way you will accept the lie; to squeal with delight when the stolen quarter appears; to vote for Mommy and Daddy when they promise to steal another.

Alas, there is no Tooth Fairy, and there is no Tooth Fairy Government. If you still believe in either one, you need to grow up.

We have run out of other people's quarters, and it is time that Mommy and Daddy quit playing make believe and tell you where quarters really come from. The capitalists make them; or we would if the government would get out of our way.

Wealth is produced; it is the product of someone's labor.

To claim an entitlement to someone else's labor is to enslave them, to make *their* person *your* property. And slavery is immoral, whether it is done by an individual, a corporation, or a government.

Enslaving our most productive capitalists – i.e. "taxing the rich" – is not only immoral, it is stupid. It prevents those most able to create the most wealth from doing so. It means less quarters when we desperately need more of them.

The Tooth Fairy socialists have never understood where quarters come from. They give it no more thought than does the child peeking under his pillow hoping another one will somehow appear.

We should love both our children and our socialists, but we shouldn't let either of them run the country.

Free Markets

Opponents of free market capitalism ritually object to its perceived unfairness. This is not a deficiency in economic literacy, it is a deficiency in vocabulary – "free" and "fair" are two different concepts.

In economic exchange, "fair" is a subjective term; what is fair to one is seen as unfair to another. It is an emotional response made after the fact. "Free" is an objective term; it is an observable attribute of the process of exchange.

Freedom in economic exchange is the absence of 3rd party interference with the will of the principals. Any voluntary exchange is inherently fair, as neither party would complete a transaction against his/her own self-interest.

Our country was founded upon the principle of self-sovereignty; we are a nation of 300 million Kings and Queens. Kings and Queens do not accept boundaries placed upon them by the minions they appoint to administer governmental affairs.

Libertarians believe in free markets, and free market capitalism in its purest forms. It is our point of departure from many Republicans and most Democrats on matters of economic philosophy.

We reject all forms of coercion on principle, and we recognize that economic liberty and personal liberty are inseparable. The regulated economy only serves the interest of the regulators. Putting a different color jersey on the regulators each election cycle does not liberate human action in economic exchange.

Anti-capitalists point to labor abuses of the 19th century industrial revolution as proof of the essential immorality of capitalism. They celebrate the creation of the Department of Labor in 1913 as the beginning of the enlightenment, the dawn of the age of regulated state capitalism, where public interest trumps self-interest in matters of economics and commerce.

They have it wrong. Self-interest *is* the public interest. Consider this list of goods invented during the century *preceding* the establishment of the regulatory state:

Automobile, telephone, elevator, escalator, refrigeration, anesthesia, airplane, camera, motion picture, air conditioning, fiber optics, dishwasher, sewing machine, fax machine, gasoline, hydrogen fuel cell, light bulb, electric motor, railway, steamships, bicycle, radio, plastic.

Would the critics of capitalism prefer to live without the products it has given us? I think not. Organized societies of humans had existed for thousands of years before 1800, so why do you think that this explosion of invention occurred in this place and in that time? What happened to unleash a century of unparalleled prosperity, charity, and improvement in living standards?

America happened, that's what.

For the first time in history, government was limited by liberty instead of the other way around. For the first time in history, individuals truly owned the fruits of their own labors. Innovation, ingenuity, and industry were liberated in the human spirit and the result was prosperity beyond imagination. It was no accident; we were not just lucky, our prosperity was the deliberate consequence of our liberty.

Along the way, we abolished slavery, institutionalized charity, extended life expectancy, established a middle class, and introduced the dynamic of economic upward mobility. Yes, there were abuses, as there are in any human endeavor.

That was then. Now we live in a different age – the age of regulated state capitalism. What will our 21st century statists list as their greatest inventions – Credit Default Swaps? Sub-prime mortgages? The Internet kill switch?

Free markets select winners and losers on merit alone. The order goes to the best supplier, however the customer defines best. The employee joins up with the best place to work, however he/she defines best.

It is the consumer who wields absolute power in the free market, not the producer. Each dollar has the same market power, regardless of what color hand is holding it – or gender, age, sexual preference, or physical state.

The consumer decides what products will be sold and at what price. The consumer rewards success and punishes failure.

Producers only survive and thrive when they give consumers what they want. This is the only reliable expression of "the public good". Those who can't or won't please the consumer, fail; failure is essential to the capitalist system, as it redistributes productive assets to those better able to meet the needs of consumers. Markets redistribute wealth more efficiently than any government could.

The State-regulated market transfers power to the producers and their regulators. Consumers are deprived of choice and their power to choose. The State places its self-interest above the individual consumer's self-interest, and the State defines "the public good" in collusion with large and powerful producers seeking to insulate themselves from open competition in the market. Regulation, by its nature, stifles innovation, protects the bad operator, and constrains the good.

It is delusional to imagine that State regulators are morally superior to producers and consumers, that their motivations are nobler. Statists and socialists who rail against individual self-interest are the most self-interested of all, demanding that millions of us comply with their own preferences, whims, and fancies against our wishes. They will not tolerate choices that deviate from their own; their idea of diversity is for us to act on their beliefs. When they can't convince, they coerce.

They produce nothing, and yet they dictate what is to be produced and what is to be consumed. They substitute their rigid ideologies for the rightful self-interest of the producer and consumer in voluntary exchange. They suppress innovation, ingenuity, and industry, and then curse the very free enterprise system they have just disarmed.

The statists are not a necessary annoyance, they are an affront to the dignity of every free man and woman and everyone who aspires to be free.

In the economic history of the world, progress has been achieved by the disruptors, not by the State's regulators. We will not unleash another era of unimaginable prosperity until we liberate our markets, and we will not liberate our markets until we dismantle our regulatory bureaucracy. We can begin this November, and we must.

Dr. Tim's Campaign Stump Speech

I call it Tooth Fairy Government: they steal your quarter, put it under their kid's pillow and then make believe they made the world 25 cents richer.

No one believes in the Tooth Fairy except for young children and old socialists. We should love our children and our socialists, but we shouldn't let either of them run the country.

My name is Tim Nerenz, and I want to be your Congressman.

Not your mommy. Not your daddy. Not your doctor, banker, car salesman, teacher, pastor, union steward, or weather forecaster.

I don't care if you are a Democrat, Republican, Libertarian, Independent, or only vote on American Idol; I want to represent you in Congress. Represent, not rule.

Because most of us want government to keep us safe, protect our rights, and then leave us alone.

Leave us alone to go to work, raise our families, run our businesses, build our communities, educate our children, practice our faith, pursue our interests, and take care of each other as we see fit.

Less government and more choices: that's my answer, what's your question?

Is it the economy, education, environment, health care, energy, jobs, drugs, guns, taxes, trade, currency, foreign relations, transportation, lifestyle, pensions, unions, social issues? You tell me what's important to you and my answer is still the same – less government for them, and more choices for you.

I won't promise a free lunch; I promise to quit stealing your lunch money.

I won't ask Nancy Pelosi how to vote; I will ask the Constitution – I keep a copy with me right here in my suit pocket at all times.

I'm not going to Washington to bring home the bacon; I'm going to Washington to shut down the slaughterhouse.

Liberty is the absence of government in choice. Government is the absence of liberty in choice. Tyranny is the absence of choice in Government.

Choose Liberty. Choose Tim, Not Tammy.

None of Your Business

President Obama is right: at some point you have made enough money. That point is called: it's-none-of-your-damn-business.

It's nobody's business how much money you make, how much you spend, what you spend it on, how much you save, how much you invest, what you invest in, how much you profit, how much you give away, and who you give it to.

It's your money, that's why.

And while we are at it, it's nobody's business what you eat, drink, smoke, drive, wear, buy, sell, grow, read, watch, shoot, carry, study, listen to, pray with, heat with, and sleep with, either.

It's your life, that's why.

These are the truths that our Declaration of Independence described as self-evident. They need no justification. This is not the United States of Mommy; you don't have to explain yourself to anyone except your spouse and your God. Certainly not to the government, the Congress, or the President, who all work for you.

Most of us would not dare talk to the boss the way our civil servants - key word servants - talk to us. And a good boss corrects his young and inexperienced employees when they don't seem to grasp the principles of the firm. So listen up.

At some point, Mr. President, you have *taken* enough of money; why don't you go away and stim on that for a while?

And at some point, Mr. President, you have *spent* enough of money; in 2010 that point is about $1.4 trillion ago.

And at some point, Mr. President, you have *borrowed* enough money; how about you just do your job from now on, and quit trying to tell us how to do ours?

In fact, Mr. President, we just think that at some point, you folks have served enough days as our elected representatives.

Because, Mr. President, you had it pretty close to right. There is a point where we indeed have had enough of something, but it isn't money.

We've had enough taxes, enough spending, enough debt, enough regulation, enough bailouts, enough unemployment, enough political correctness, enough nationalizing of industries, enough war, enough energy rationing, enough lies, enough snooping, and enough disregard for the Constitution.

The American Dream is not about owning, it is about *earning*. We are a nation of possibilities, not a nation of limits. We will earn as much or as little as *we* want, and we will make those decisions for ourselves, thank you very much.

A government that can decide when you have earned enough money can also decide when you have spent enough – on health care, education, energy, charities it does not like, opposition political parties, cars, houses, recreation, guns, and all manner of things that are the pursuit of happiness one day, felonies the next.

In America, we the people place limits on the government, not the other way around. It is our trust in liberty that makes us exceptional in the world; or did, before we elected people who were either afraid or ashamed to be exceptional.

Libertarians are not afraid of Liberty, nor are we ashamed of the prosperity, charity, and happiness it brings out in those lucky enough to live under its immunity.

Mr. President, there is no point where you have too much Liberty.

Liberty Is

You have heard me say it many times: Liberty is the absence of government in choice. It was the *absence* of government that made us a great nation.

The greatest American achievements – the abolition of slavery, the creation of the middle class, private charity, and the industrial revolution – occurred in the first American century, when government was constrained and liberty was not.

For nearly all of that century, government consumed less than 5% of national output, leaving us 95% free to act on our own volition.

It is not by accident that we raised from obscurity to become the most prosperous, the most virtuous, and the healthiest people on earth – those are the certain benefits of free market capitalism and limited government.

Conversely, the second American century was defined by the growth of government and the constraint of liberty.

It will be remembered for two world wars, the Great Depression, and a 45-year Cold War with the Soviet Union played out through various proxy conflicts around the world.

War and wealth destruction are the equally certain consequences of socialism and big government.

Just as the absence of government propelled living standards and public morality forward in the first American century, the expansion of government in the second eroded our standard of living and debased the moral underpinning of our national identity.

Government now consumes over 50% of GDP; we have become the land of the half-free and the home of the half-brave. We should quit pretending otherwise.

The socialists in both parties who perpetrated this offensive against capitalism and liberty will not accept any responsibility for their actions.

In fact, they blame liberty and capitalism for the consequences of their efforts to subvert them.

Capitalism is not the cause of our economic troubles; capitalism is the cure for our economic troubles.

Pure, free-market capitalism – unregulated, unfettered, unbowed – is the only socio-economic system compatible with Liberty and individual rights.

Voluntary exchange is the only rational means for two sovereign human beings to relate to each other; the only way for their individual rights to be respected fully.

The proper role of government in voluntary economic exchange is *absence*.

Let me state this plainly: people should be free to buy and sell any product, service, and form of labor under any mutually agreeable terms to whomever and from whomever they wish at all times – *without exception*.

This is what economic freedom means. And economic freedom is the only relevant measure of liberty in a society.

Freedom of thought and speech is meaningless without the freedom to act, and freedom to act requires economic exchange.

Personal liberty and economic liberty are but two sides of the same coin; you can't pretend to keep one while throwing the other away.

Do not lose sight of this fact: every dollar spent by government was taken by force from someone who earned it. That person was deprived of his liberty to spend, save, or gift that dollar as he sees fit.

The moral offense of deprivation of economic liberty negates any proffer of "public good" offered as justification.

Need does not justify the taking; not for the looter, the rapist, the thug, or the government.

We forget that even greater good would have been done with the private spending of that same dollar.

It would have generated employment better than any federal stimulus bill.

It would have purchased better health care than the government can provide.

It would have permitted a charity to change a person's life more than any government welfare program ever did.

It would have been invested in a venture that was literally sustainable, not just figuratively so.

Is there a single one of you so foolish you would allow me to take away half your income to spend as I see fit?

Then why on earth would you permit me to do it as your Congressman?

There are 535 members of the Congress and Senate; every single one of them is less qualified than you to decide how you should live your life.

You are the world's foremost expert on the subject of pursuit of your happiness. I am not going to Washington to pursue mine; I am going to Washington to guarantee that you have the right to pursue yours.

FLIP

It is easy to remember the acronym FLIP: Free trade, Limited government, Individual Liberty, and Private property.

The libertarian political philosophy is adequately explained using just these four basic principles. And working the acronym FLIP backwards from right to left, each one builds upon the other in sequence.

You alone are the owner of your person and the fruits of your labor – that is private property.

You alone are entitled to dispose of your person and property as you see fit – that is individual liberty.

The only just purpose of government is to protect your rights to life, liberty, and property - that is limited government.

And the only just transaction between free sovereign persons is voluntary exchange – that is free trade.

Is there any moral alternative? Does someone else own your person and the fruits of your labor? Does someone else have the right to dispose of your person and property? Should the government have the power to set its own limits? Should someone else hold veto power over your voluntary exchange?

Of course not; yet those are *exactly* the tenets of the socialist progressive ideology which has transformed our politics over the past century. Government no longer exists to protect the rights of individuals; rather to impose the will of the majority political Party upon all citizens. The language of liberty has been corrupted; its meanings twisted to fit opposite aims.

Trade is *not* free when it is controlled by the government through regulation, licensure, subsidy, preference, prohibition, monopoly, tariff, quota, and taxation.

A government is *not* limited that ignores the Constitution, seizes half of the nation's output and spends it to manipulate markets, change foreign regimes, redistribute earnings, harass citizens, and prosecute victimless crimes.

Individual liberty does *not* exist when government tells us what we can eat, drink, smoke, wear, own, shoot, say, buy, sell, rent, drive, read, see, teach, display, hear, and earn.

Property is *not* private when the government can devalue it, confiscate it, assert a public right to it, transfer it to others by decree, and prohibit its voluntary exchange.

You have heard me say it many times; things are not so complicated when you know what you believe.

And what do you believe - do you believe that you alone are the rightful owner of your person and property? Do you believe that government should protect your rights, and be constrained from imposing the beliefs of others upon you?

Are you a FLIP person?

If so, then ask yourself this question: which political Party has stood resolute in defense of these four principles – Free Trade, Limited Government, Individual Liberty, and Private Property? Which Party has refused to compromise these principles in the face of political expediency, majority opposition, media ridicule, and national crisis?

We Libertarians hope that you will find us to be that Party – the Party of Principle, just as we say we are. We hope you will join us, vote for our candidates, work in our campaigns, come to our events, donate to our cause, and help us to fight for the principles we believe in – FLIP.

We will respect your decision gratefully or gracefully, as the case may be. Our purpose is not to convince you to change your principles; it is to provide you the opportunity to vote for them.

You Might Be A Libertarian

"Keep your money, keep your guns, keep your stash – any two out of three and you might be a libertarian; all three and you ought to join the Libertarian Party".

This slightly irreverent pitch was how I was introduced to the Libertarian Party many years ago. It doesn't mean we advocate tax cheating, violating gun laws, and taking drugs, but it is useful shorthand to describe the three basic strands of libertarianism: economic liberty, constitutional government, and personal liberty.

Most Libertarians start out from one of those three reference points and then discover that all three are inseparable. Personal liberty and economic liberty are two sides of the same coin, and the Constitution constrains the government from taking it away.

Libertarianism (small letter "l") is a political philosophy that places Liberty – the absence of government in choice – as its first principle. This was the bold American ideal, the noble purpose for which our nation was formed, the reason we prospered. It was radical at first, then mainstream, and is now radical again.

George Washington used the phrases "liberty of conscience" and "immunity of citizenship" when describing the uniquely virtuous relationship between the American people, their government, and the Constitution that protects the former from the latter. That is eloquence that can not be improved upon.

And I believe that Liberty is still the first principle of most Americans, whether they identify themselves as Republicans, Democrats, Libertarians, or Independents; and especially if they are political agnostics.

Most Americans want government to keep us safe, protect our rights, and then leave us alone to live our lives as we see fit. Most of us do not want government to tell us what we can and can't do, what is good for us and bad for us – we have many other sources much better qualified to give us guidance in these matters.

Most of us do not want to criminalize our neighbors' choices; but neither do we want to pay for them. We treasure natural diversity, and we hate forced conformity. Look at how we dress, decorate our homes, accessorize our cars – we will spare no expense to be different. You have to confiscate our money and use it to impose uniformity upon us by force, we won't accept it voluntarily.

Most Americans want to live a Dutch Treat life - each making our own choices and paying our own way. Equality of opportunity is a buffet, while equality of outcome is prison food. This is a buffet nation; we hate prison food.

Most of us want a stout defense of our nation, but we do not want to defend any others; and we don't wish to impose our will on them by threat of force. We want to buy and sell things with other countries, not keep them dependent on our foreign aid. We want our troops brought home - defending us here, not fighting abroad for years in undeclared wars where there is no clear strategy for victory.

There are libertarian Republicans and libertarian Democrats, although it is getting more and more difficult to find them. Most Libertarians started out as one or the other of these and then decided to drop the second half of the label when they became unwelcome in their own party. Libertarian independents aren't welcome in either party – except, of course, on election day, when even candidate Obama promises to cut their taxes.

But you are all welcome in the Libertarian Party. Whether your thing is personal liberty, economic liberty, or constitutional restraint of government, you will find that the Libertarian Party is the Party of Principle, just as we claim. Today's Republicans and Democrats bear little resemblance to the parties of Goldwater and Kennedy; the divergence began in the late 1960's and led to the creation of the LP in 1971. We haven't changed; they did.

In my congressional campaign, I have used the acronym FLIP – Free trade, Limited government, Individual liberty, and Private property – to convey to people the basic pillars of libertarian political philosophy. It is easy to remember, and more respectable than "keep your stash", especially when children are present.

Does FLIP describe your political philosophy? Have you taken the World's Smallest Political Quiz? You can find it at

TOOTH FAIRY GOVERNMENT

www.theadvocates.org/quizp/index.html and it only takes a minute.

You might be a Libertarian and not even know it. That's how we all started out.

The Real Minimum Wage Is Zero

The real minimum wage is zero. That's what many more people will be earning soon thanks to the Wisconsin state legislature's vote to increase the state minimum wage by 17%, to $7.60 per hour.

You don't ever hear an economist suggest minimum wage increases - they know better. Less than 5% of people earn the minimum wage; it is essentially a training wage, and is paid for entry level jobs where people learn basic job skills and then move up the proverbial ladder. Making the first step higher makes it more difficult for people to start the climb, not easier.

The argument for minimum wage is that corporations must be forced to pay a "living wage" and would not do so voluntarily. That is ridiculous, considering that 95% of jobs pay higher than minimum wage without any legal requirement to do so.

Everyone who works is being paid less than what their employer thinks they are worth, and more than what they think they are worth. If the employer doesn't think your value is more than your pay, you won't have a job; if you don't think you are paid more than your worth, you will change jobs.

This is basic economics; perhaps instead of a minimum wage law, we should enact a minimum economics law that would force legislators to take a class or at least read a book.

A law that says a job is worth $7.60 an hour does not make it so. If the job is worth $7.60, it will pay $7.60. If the job is worth less than $7.60, it will disappear. Unfortunately, our legislators just voted to make a lot of jobs disappear.

What Comes After Stupid?

One of my previous health care posts was titled "Quit Talking Stupid", but I should have stopped at "Quit Talking". This week, the Senate will vote on a new Health Care Bill that redefines stupid.

The "cost" of this bill is scored by CBO at $849 billion, and CBO estimates it would reduce the deficit by $130 billion. That is stupid squared.

Let's give just one minute of thought to those two statements. The CBO number is a net number; that is, all of the new costs *less* all six of its new taxes = $849 billion of net additional government spending. That *increases* the deficit by, duh, $849 billion.

And the $849 billion "cost" assumes a $500 billion gutting of Medicare in the out years; as if that would ever actually happen. The bill creates a panel to provide for "adjustments" if necessary – yeah, like when 100 million old people rush the Russell Senate Office Building with pitchforks, ropes, and torches. So let's drop that lie and call it $1.35 trillion of double-down stupid.

An earlier Senate version got to its equally stupid CBO score of $827 billion by cutting doctor's fees by 25% and leaving them there. That must still be in this new one, as it was a $257 billion sprinkling of fairy dust which will also *never* happen. Tres Stupid. And now we are talking $1.5 trillion.

To repeat my past warnings of ENRON accounting in the CBO scoring of these bills, the new and improved Harry Reid Bill puts off most benefits until 2014, so they count 10 years of new taxes and only 5 years of paid benefits. Stupid times four.

Take 10 years of taxes and a full 10 years of benefit costs and the real net cost of a decade under this new health care system is over $2 trillion. That is the number that we need to double to account for every single government welfare program costing twice as much as we think it will.

Still want government health care? Ok, but talk $4 trillion of the stuff, and tell us where you will get the money from. Tax the rich? Already included. Increase Medicare taxes? Them, too.

Forced premiums – ditto. Employer payroll taxes – yup. Tax premiums – way ahead of you. Tax flex savings – c'mon, man!

Remember all that talk about making our health care system more affordable? Yeah, well, this new one is so expensive that they had to add in a subsidy to families making up to $88,000 to help them pay all the new taxes and fees you are going to get stuck with. Chad Stupidcinco.

And the coup de stupid? Our current system, with all of its problems, covers 90% of legal American citizens who want to purchase health insurance but can't. The new Senate Bill increases coverage to 94%. What?? We are about to throw away the best health care system in the world and bust the bank by over $4 trillion to increase coverage by a measly 4%, and that doesn't happen for five more years.

This is stupid to the 10th power. It is unbearably stupid. Now I know why texters have so many different ways to abbreviate laughing hysterically out loud.

Don't even bother to read the 2,074 page bill. Whatever the Senate passes will get tossed aside along with last month's House bill when Nancy and Harry write up a brand new conference bill that will be even more stupid than the two versions they throw out. And then 100 different agencies will write up rules and regulations on a whim – like rationing mammograms, for instance.

Besides, you don't need to read it to make up your mind, you just need to ask yourself one question: if it is as good for you as they claim, then why do they have to lie this much to get their own members to vote for it?

They *know* this will suck. I believe them; you should too.

TOOTH FAIRY GOVERNMENT

Defending The American Dream

I call it Tooth Fairy Government – they take your quarter, stick it under their kids' pillows, and make believe the world is 25 cents richer.

Now, the only people who believe in the tooth fairy are young children and old socialists. We should love our children, and we should love our socialists, but we should not let either of them run the country.

Like most of you, I did not set out to be a radical. Like most of you, this is my first crack at being an activist. Like most of you, my American Dream did not have a scene with me standing in front of thousands of people fighting to take our country back.

But then I never thought I would be living in a NASCAR republic. A NASCAR republic is where every time you look up the leaders of the pack just took another hard left turn and crashed us into the wall.

A half century of those left turns have made *us* the radicals now, and all we did was stand firm in one place.

A place where government is limited and liberty is not; a place where government needs our permission to act, not the other way around; a place where Government is our servant, not our master. A place where we own the mansion and government is our Cabana Boy.

And our Cabana Boy has a job description; it is called the Constitution. The black ink tells Cabana Boy what he can do; and the white space belongs to us. Problem is, our Cabana Boy doesn't read.

Our Cabana Boy forgot which of us is the servant, and which is the master. Our Cabana Boy tells us what we can and can't do. Our Cabana Boy tells us how much of our own money he will let us keep. Our Cabana Boy steals from our children and our grandchildren.

So what do we do with a Cabana Boy who does not know his place? We fire him, that's what. And that is exactly what we should do this November – sack the whole miserable mess of them and start over.

Start over with people who have read the Constitution; who know the difference between the black ink and the white space. People who will represent, not rule. People who understand it is not their money.

People who are not afraid to be a great nation; not shamed of being better than the others. The Socialists in Washington think you have too much money, too much energy, too much freedom, too many guns, even too much health care.

They want you to surrender *your* liberty so *they* can run everything, just like they do over in Europe. We are here today to stop them. This isn't a partisan event. We are not the Party of No. We are the Party of *Hell No!*

Do you want to give them your money? Do you want to give them your guns? Do you want to give them your health care, your energy, your Liberty? I say Hell No!

Europe is all we hear about these days – Europe has high speed rail, Europe has cap and trade, Europe has national industries, Europe has unions, Europe has government health care, Europe has VAT tax. Europe, Europe, Europe. Marcia, Marcia, Marcia.

Let me tell you something: Europe sucks.

They make 20% less than we do. They pay double the taxes we do. They're unemployment rate is twice as high as ours. They live in tiny little apartments; they drive tiny little cars, and they ride little bikes with little baskets on them. They wear tiny little glasses and tiny little speedos. They still pay attention to Al Gore.

And we are supposed to give up our American Dream for that? Why? Because they live longer than us? That's not living.

I don't know about you, but I don't care how old they are in Belgium. I would rather live free for 79 years than be a slave to the state for 81.

Thank you for caring enough to join me here today.

Corporatista!

You can't be for jobs and against the corporations that create them; you can't hate profits and love the abundance they provide. Pick your side.

As Congress prepares to shovel out another steaming load of faux-stimulus cynically labeled a "jobs" bill, it is useful to remind ourselves of why they think we need one.

When Nancy Pelosi took control of the House in January of 2007, the Dow was closing in on 14,000 and unemployment was at 4.5%.

She has not uttered a syllable as Speaker that has not been anti-corporation, anti-profit, and anti-capitalist. It only took a few months into her reign for the recession to begin.

No mystery there - she promised to increase corporate income taxes, hike capital gains taxes, confiscate repatriated profits, ration energy, impose unions without elections, tax carbon, regulate wages and benefits, impose price controls, increase inheritance taxes, nationalize banks, autos, insurance, mortgages, credit, and health care. Business optimism plummeted – imagine that.

Then President Obama was sworn in and proceeded to publicly flog banks, doctors, hospitals, insurance companies, tobacco companies, oil companies, hedge funds, drug companies, automobile companies, dealers, bondholders, Walmart, Defense contractors, coal companies, their customers, Las Vegas, and every small business that makes over $250,000 per year. I'm sure I missed some; I don't watch MSNBC.

The collateral damage of Nancy and Tammy's War on Capitalism is more than 7 million Americans who have lost their jobs. The President still doesn't get it; just last week he called for new subsidies for his pet industry, saying the government needs to "create a system of incentives to make clean energy profitable." As if.

Government can't "make" anything profitable; all it can do is increase taxes on profitable firms to subsidize unprofitable ones, helping neither. If I scalp off a piece of George Clooney's face and staple it on to mine, we *both* get uglier; we don't spread the handsome around. Econ 101 for Hollywood liberals.

Occasionally, someone calls me a Corporatist and expects me to flinch and retreat in contrition. They got the wrong boy; in fact, you may call me *Corporatista* – radical, unrepentant, and proud defender of free market capitalism.

When the Pick 'N' Save makes a profit, you don't get screwed; you get food. So eat it, all you socialists who think profits and corporations are evil. The food, I mean.

In fact, everything you have only exists because somebody made a buck off it. No profits, no stuff; no corporations, no jobs. And no taxes, no government, no contributions to charities and non-profits. We are all C*orporatistas*.

Recently, I saw a group of activists with big buttons that read: *Profits Have No Place In Health Care.* What a remarkably stupid idea. Without profits, they wouldn't even have the buttons. When you remove everything that was made for a profit from health care, all that is left is a nun feeling your forehead. I'll take my chances with the MRI, thank you.

There are millions of corporations; 90% of them have less than 50 employees. Most are family-owned; many more act like they are. Small corporations are the engine of job creation; the source of innovation; the incubator for new products, services, technologies, and ideas. They earn their profits, they don't depend on government bailouts and subsidies like the too-big-not-to-fail corporate welfare queens do.

And Wisconsin is home to some of the best corporations in the world – small, medium, and large. Our most formidable threat is not the workers in the sweatshops of Mexico or China; it is the government bureaucrats sitting in cubicles in Madison and Washington D.C. They are taxing and regulating us into extinction.

Last week I was told of a recent study which found that only 8% of the Obama administration's appointees have any business experience – the lowest percentage ever. If accurate, that explains why they don't know what they are doing.

TOOTH FAIRY GOVERNMENT

If they would ask someone who does, we would tell them: You can't be for jobs and against the corporations that create them. Markets work imperfectly, but they work. Just get out of the way and let them.

That's it. There is nothing complicated about sound capitalist economic policy; every kid who ever had a paper route or lemonade stand gets it. It is *un-sound* socialist economic policy that is impossible to comprehend.

And there is a good reason you can't make sense of it; it makes no sense.

Voluntary Exchange

There are only three ways to get what you want. You can exchange for it, you can steal it, or you can beg for someone to give it to you.

Exchange is noble, stealing is immoral, and begging is dehumanizing. There is a definite pecking order of desirability among the three alternatives.

In the free market, goods and services are exchanged between buyer and seller at a price that is determined through direct negotiation between the two parties to the exchange. The price is necessarily fair, for both sides need to benefit from the exchange or it will not take place. Any exchange is thus moral.

Government doesn't work that way. It steals from one person when it taxes, and it dispenses the loot to someone else who has successfully begged for the benefit received. The terms need not be fair, as they are set by the government without the concurrence of other parties to the transactions. The taking is immoral, and the dispensing is dehumanizing.

That is why markets are a better choice than government in all but a few instances. We need government to provide national defense, enforce contracts, build roads, maintain a currency, all sorts of things that benefit all citizens and could not be purchased through private exchanges.

But for most things, markets are more efficient than government, and markets are more responsive to changes in wants and needs of the public. Markets are less prone to corruption, and are better able to weed out incompetence and failure.

Markets are also more democratic. Each transaction is a vote, a determination of value among those competing for your purchasing power. The fortunes of Pepsi and Coke are determined by a billion choices of a dollar each – Bill Gates gets one vote per can, no more than a poor day laborer in Peru.

Pepsi and Coke must compete for your purchase of each can of soda; they also compete for your investment dollar. Millions of investors decide whether Pepsi or Coke is a better company to invest in, the CEO's of each company are powerless over the

TOOTH FAIRY GOVERNMENT

price of their stock. You will decide what a share of Coke is worth, you and some other person who will sell you their share at that price.

The advantage of a market system is that power is spread out over millions of people, instead of being concentrated in the hands of a few, as is the case in government. This is important because people make mistakes.

Think about banking. When a local bank president makes a mistake, the worst that can happen is one bank will fail – one out of hundreds of thousands. When the Chairman of the Federal Reserve makes a mistake, the entire banking system fails.

Human error is the reason that the government bailouts are such a bad idea. A few legislators and bureaucrats have too much power; their mistakes will not just impact a firm, they will impact the whole global economy. No matter how bright and well-intentioned the individuals are, they are going to make mistakes – we all do.

The market had already voted on the GM bailout long before Congress did. Car buyers decided to buy other products, and investors decided to buy other stocks. Millions of people decided not to exchange their labor (wages) for a GM product or a share of GM stock.

So GM went to the government to get by begging for stolen dollars what it could not earn in voluntary exchange and competition.

And the government obliged, dispensing billions of dollars taken from the very same citizens who had already said "NO!" to GM products and stock shares. GM got billions of our dollars anyway, and they got to keep the cars – who wouldn't rather deal with the government than the market?

Once GM showed us how it is done, now everyone is lining up at the trough in D.C. with hat in hand, groveling shamelessly for favors from those who control the dispensation of funds confiscated from those of us who still earn it the noble way – by free exchange in the market.

Brace yourself. This will not be over any time soon.

Constitution of Convenience

Democrats who couldn't be bothered with the Constitution while nationalizing health care have now discovered it is a useful thing to beat Arizona over the head with.

While it is encouraging to know that some liberals have embraced the 4th Amendment, it is disappointing that they skipped over the 1st and 2nd to get there, and then stopped reading before the got to the 9th and 10th.

Am I the only one that sees the irony in liberal outrage over non-citizens *possibly* being asked to produce identification, while at the same time they (Senator Chuck Schumer) propose *mandatory* implants of bio-chips into citizens to track our financial and health histories?

This is the kind of bizarre contradiction that is created when power replaces principle and representation turns to rule. It's not that Libertarians object to protecting individuals from their government; we have been driving that bus for 40 years. It's just that we haven't seen Democrats riding shotgun for quite some time.

But there is no high principle motivating the socialists here. This has nothing to do with concern for the welfare of illegal immigrants or with respect for the Constitution; it is all about power and control.

Don't be fooled - what the D.C. socialists are really outraged about is that a state (Arizona) had the audacity to act on its own rather than take its marching orders from Washington. Not just any state, but one with a woman governor who isn't a Democrat, if we want to be honest about what really gets under their skin.

Will the liberal Democrats go berserk if Wisconsin passes a law enforcing mandatory health insurance when that kicks in? Oh, no…..that's *different*. Would they forego their 16,000 new IRS agents to beef up border security so that states don't have to take matters into their own hands? Dream on. Will they call for a boycott of any state that checks concealed carry permits? Oops, wrong Amendment.

TOOTH FAIRY GOVERNMENT

Empires can not allow their colonies to assert sovereignty, and we have lapsed back into empire. The capital has moved from London to Washington, but both are light years removed from the reality imposed on us subjects out here in the hinterlands. They take more and more of our money, and they give us more and more rules to follow.

King Barack and Queen Nancy are trying to stomp out a growing rebellion among the colonies – opting out of health care, tackling illegal immigration, rejecting federal drug laws, setting marriage criteria, protecting gun rights, organizing tea parties, and other unthinkable acts of insubordination.

To all those rebellious states and uppity citizens, I say "good on ya". And to all the liberals who have come around to the idea that government should stay out of the illegal immigrants' business, I say "congratulations". Now just add citizens and legal immigrants to your list, and you just might be a Libertarian.

The first American Revolution was fought with bullets and blood; the second is being fought with ballots and blogs. Arizona is just a skirmish along the way to restoring our Constitution and replacing our empire with a representative republic once again.

A Fair Tax

While we may disagree about how much government should tax and spend, we can all agree that our system of taxation needs to be reformed.

The current tax system is so complicated that Americans spend over $400 billion each year in compliance and filing costs alone. Even the IRS can not properly interpret their own rules; they are regularly overturned in appeals.

The tax code is the mechanism by which political favors are doled out – punitive tax treatments for enemies and tax breaks and loopholes for favored campaign donors. Subsidies, preferences, and fines distort the functioning of markets and severely limit economic growth.

The most damaging thing about our tax system is that it provides exactly the wrong economic incentives. It punishes work, saving, investment, and success, while it rewards spending, borrowing, and failure.

When new tax increases take effect in January, we will have the highest corporate taxes in the world, and a system that favors imports while it discourages exports. It drives investment capital and jobs overseas; businesses are leaving to avoid punitive taxes, and jobs are leaving with them.

Many alternatives have been proposed to the current failed system of taxation; the one that I support is called the FairTax. It is simple, it is eminently fair, and it is very easy to enact immediately.

The FairTax is a uniform consumption tax embedded into the price of all retail purchases. Under the fair tax, there would be no more withholding of taxes from your paycheck, and all other federal taxes are eliminated. Abolish the IRS and repeal the 16th amendment. No more filing, no more forms, no audits, no need to cheat and finagle and fudge numbers – just buy the things you need and want and marvel at how many of them will suddenly be made in the USA again.

Everyone will pay taxes proportional to their spending, and no consumption will be excluded; that is both fair and neutral in terms of market functioning and investment returns. It levels the playing field with foreign producers of goods and services.

Rather than describe the details of the FairTax proposal here, I will provide the link to this website and encourage you to read about it yourself: www.Fairtax.org. Many in Congress already support it, as do many prominent economists.

In an ideal world, i.e. one conceived and wisely ruled by Libertarians, there would be no need for compulsory taxes, and the footprint of government would be so limited that the method of taxation would be of small consequence. That day is unfortunately far off.

In the meantime, we can't wait to reform the method of taxation until we have reduced the amount of taxes needed to fund a government of limited scope. As the old saw goes, Best should not be the enemy of Better.

FairTax is not a partisan issue. Regardless of how much you think we should be taxed, or what you think tax dollars should be spent on, reforming our system of taxation to make it fair, efficient, simple, and globally competitive is in everyone's interest.

I have made it an issue of substance in my campaign, and I call upon Tammy and all other challengers in the District 2 race to either join me in endorsing FairTax or to propose their better idea.

A Sensible Foreign Policy

A sensible American foreign policy has only three parts: 1) we will buy your stuff, 2) we will sell you our stuff, and 3) we will obliterate you if you attack us.

There is no part four – all those not-sensible things that we do now. - foreign aid, military interventions, foreign basing, NATO, UN, WTO, IMF, World Bank, NAFTA, OAS, sanctions, tariffs, defense treaties, and any "accord" named after a city – Kyoto, Doha, Rio, that kind of thing.

The three sensible parts make us more prosperous and safer; that should be the goal of any foreign policy and that should be the extent of America's foreign policy goals. The internationalists' ideal of a collectively ordered world has increased bloodshed and driven poor countries into even deeper poverty.

The *only* way Americans can really help developing countries develop is to buy things that they make and to sell them things they need.

Free trade creates jobs (real ones) both there and here; and jobs are the only path to prosperity. Prosperity, in turn, is the only immunization from insurrection and warfare. A million Waldorf salads have been wasted over decades of useless conferences whose purpose was to deny that simple truth.

The solution to global poverty is free trade, not foreign aid. People trade, not governments; and we should simply let them. And a proper free trade agreement is a blank sheet of paper. It's all downhill once the lawyers start putting ink on it.

Capitalism is inherently compassionate; free trade allows people to rise above the circumstances of their birth and realize their full economic potential. It rewards ambition and talent, and it discriminates only on the basis of merit and accomplishment. Markets do what governments can't; lift people up.

Whenever nations trust free markets, living standards rise. South Korea, Singapore, Hong Kong, Chile, New Zealand, Ireland, Taiwan, China, India – there is no shortage of evidence over the past half-century. We used to trust markets once ourselves; it is how we got all this wealth we are now so busy squandering.

There is nothing compassionate about meddling internationalists keeping people perpetually poor and dependent on foreign aid. There is nothing noble about making meaningless gestures designed to ease our own guilt and shame; in fact, it is the hypocrisy of meaningless gestures that creates the guilt and shame. If you choose to marinate yourself in self-loathing, you go right ahead, but I would prefer to actually help lift someone out of poverty, by trading with them.

The third part of my foreign policy prescription is an obliterating force. The idea is simple enough; if a state attacks us, we will destroy it. No exceptions, no negotiations, no sanctions, no stern letter from Hillary, no mulligans. The phrase "hell to pay" is appropriate, given the magnificent capabilities of our military.

Note that I advocate only self-defense, not offensive attacks, not military interventions at the invitation of other nations, and the defense of other countries, Canada and Mexico excepted. Germany can defend herself, so can Japan, Korea, Taiwan, Afghanistan, Iraq, and the 100 other countries where we maintain bases, stage troops, or are bound by defense treaties.

Trade with us and we prosper together; attack us and you die. That's the deal.

A Strong Defense

People often confuse Libertarians' opposition to unconstitutional military interventions abroad with a general opposition to national defense.

While there is a wide spectrum of positions held by principled Libertarians on matters of war and peace, there is no inherent conflict between advocating a strong national defense on one hand and opposing overseas military interventions on the other.

What military footprint would be necessary to repel any invasion, to respond to any attack on our soil by a foreign power, and to protect our access to international sea and air trade routes? That is how much military we need.

How much more military do we have that we do *not* need – forces that defend Japan, South Korea, Europe, and Latin America? How much more to maintain major bases on over 50 countries located on all the continents? How much more to maintain a ready invasion force capable of fighting two major conflicts overseas simultaneously? That, unfortunately, is what we have.

Our military should only be used to deter aggression against our sovereignty, to repel invasions, to retaliate against attacks. It should not be used to change regimes, to occupy territory of other nations, to "send a message", to defend regimes we like, or vague missions like "nation building" or "peace keeping". Our military are war fighters who serve voluntarily, and we are grateful to have the best in the world.

These war fighters should be sent to war only by Congressional declaration. It is supreme cowardice for politicians to send American citizens to die while hiding behind vague resolutions whose only purpose is to take credit or provide cover later, depending on how things work out.

An overwhelming retaliatory capability is the best guarantee that we would never have to use it. Requiring a Congressional declaration adds an important deliberative step before sending American forces into combat. We have engaged our forces in 10 conflicts since World War II without a Congressional declaration of war.

While reasonable people can disagree over many particulars of Defense and military policy, I think most of us would have a common understanding of defense versus offense. Our national right to self-defense is similar to our individual right. We are justified in shooting our neighbor when he breaks into our house and heads towards our kids' room with a gun; we are not justified in going over to his house and shooting him because we are afraid he might shoot someone else's kids someday.

A stronger defense would cost less than half of what we spend on our military today. The Department of Defense is a bloated bureaucracy of the worst order, and drastic reform is urgently needed to streamline procurement, define accountability, and dismantle the corporate welfare system that is perpetuated by both government and industry. My doctoral dissertation examined Defense Department procurement practices, so I'm not just guessing about these things.

We can have a *stronger* national defense, bring our troops back home, and cut spending by over $300 billion per year. Neither the Republicans (save Ron Paul) nor the Democrats support any substantive change in our military posture. They are all married to the military/industrial complex and committed to a militaristic foreign policy priority.

Which foreign policy priority of the Obama administration is fundamentally different than those of the Bush administration? Which of the countries holding our foreign policy hostage – i.e. North Korea, Iran, Iraq, Afghanistan, Pakistan, Cuba, Venezuela, the broader Middle East – poses a credible military threat to our sovereign territory? Are they problems? Yes. Our problems? No.

But what of the terrorist threat? Terrorism is a very real and very difficult threat to our safety and Liberty that we must face squarely. I would suggest that the U.S. response to the Somali pirate incident was appropriate. Our actions were lethal and proportionate, and if the lack of further incidents is any indication, effective. When Libya was found to have sponsored a specific terrorist act against the United States in the 1980's, two missiles into Col. Quadafi's tent and he booted the terrorists out of his country.

These are the kinds of responses to terrorism that are effective.

We can not invade every country from which a terrorist attack is launched or plotted. A strong defense policy must include an effective intelligence apparatus and a capability of proportional response when local governments are incapable or unwilling to confront terrorists operating within their territory.

A Woman's Right To Choose

Democrats feel entitled to a majority of women's votes because of their noisy proclamations of belief in a "a woman's right to choose". Crock.

What about a woman's right to choose what schools her children will attend?

What about a woman's right to choose her health insurance?

What about a woman's right to choose what kind of gun to own? How to carry it?

What about a woman's right to choose what kind of car she drives? How many? What she tows behind them?

What about a woman's right to choose whether or not to smoke, what to smoke, and where to smoke it?

What about a woman's right to choose whether or not to join a union?

What about a woman's right to choose whether or not to recycle?

What about a woman's right to choose how much energy she consumes, and what she uses it for?

What about a woman's right to choose which charities she gives her money to?

What about a woman's right to raise and discipline her children as she believes proper?

What about a woman's right to choose what substances she puts into her own body and for what purposes?

What about a woman's right to choose how much of her income to save, spend, invest, gift, and pass on to her heirs?

What about a woman's right to choose which radio and television stations she will listen to and watch?

What about a woman's right to choose to start a business and operate it the way she thinks best? To hire who she wants? To pay them compensation she believes to be fair?

What about a woman's right to choose to access energy sequestered on public lands?

What about a woman's right to choose what medicines to use and what medical treatments to seek out for herself and her family?

What about a woman's right to choose between a public pension and private retirement saving plan?

What about a woman's right to choose *not* to invest in GM, Chrysler, AIG, and the Wall Street banks?

What about a woman's right to choose what bumper stickers to put on her vehicle without being labeled a terrorist suspect?

What about a woman's right to choose to trade with people from any nation on earth?

What about a woman's right to choose for herself whether or not to increase her indebtedness?

What about a woman's right to choose whether or not to enjoy an adult beverage at 18?

Empty slogans don't fool anyone - you can't be for choice but against choices. And what high principle instructs that a woman's right to choose applies only to abortion? Do Democrats think women can only be trusted to make reproductive choices? What are they saying – that the rest of life is just too complicated for a delicate female to manage on her own? That is a demeaning view of women, if you ask me.

We Libertarians hold women in much higher regard. We think women should be free to make economic choices, health choices, moral choices, family choices, career choices, school choices, entertainment choices, security choices, travel choices, drug choices, energy choices, charity choices, and pension choices. We trust women. We respect their judgment. Apparently, not everyone does.

TOOTH FAIRY GOVERNMENT

Libertarians are pro-choice on everything, not just one thing. We are pro-choices plural, not just pro-choice singular. We are for choice from A to Z, not from Ab to Ab.

We trust both women and men to make the best choices for their own lives and families. We think that all issues are "women's issues" – not just one or two as designated by Democrat elites.

We oppose the very idea of group-think; we know that each individual person – male or female – will make choices based upon their own conscience and beliefs.

We respect those choices; that is how you show respect for the person who made them. Respect is the basis of civil order, not involuntary compliance.

Libertarians are the genuine advocates of equal rights; we do not differentiate between men's Liberty and women's Liberty.

Liberty is the absence of government in choice - all choice.

Abolish The What?

In my last post, I proposed abolishment of the Federal Reserve and the IRS; I hope I did not give anyone the impression that it was an all-inclusive list.

Democrats are a lost cause when it comes to fiscal sanity, and Republicans are math-averse – talking in platitudes about cutting taxes and reducing the deficit, but unable or unwilling to name the specific programs they would cut to get there. Libertarians are both fiscally responsible and mathematically proficient.

Let's start with the Department of Education. We send a dollar to D.C. and get 78 cents back (or less) with a boatload of stings attached. Before we federalized education we were #1 in the world; today spend twice as much per pupil and we are 17th in reading, 18th in math. Kill it before it drives us out of the top 50.

Next up, Departments of Labor and Commerce. Both exist to neutralize the power of the other - it's like suing yourself and then paying for both lawyers. Quick quiz: who is the current secretary of either department? I didn't think so. Chop, chop.

While we are at it, adios Agriculture Department. We have the internet now; we don't need the county extension agent. But wait, you say, who will divvy out the subsidies to the giant agri-businesses with no Ag Department? Bonus.

Department of Energy. Before we had a department of it, energy was cheap and plentiful and most of it was produced here. We are more dependent than ever on foreign oil while our energy costs have gone through the roof. Sayonara.

Another quick quiz: name three actual accomplishments of the United Nations. Me neither. Bye. And why are we giving out foreign aid that we borrow from the Chinese? Let them ask China for cash and cut out the middle man.

How about the Bureau of Indian Affairs? This is 2010, not 1910. The dude stuffing his money into the machines at Ho Chunk is in a lot worse shape than the dudes who are taking it out.

Department of Housing and Urban Development. 50 years and trillions of dollars later, has one Urb has been developed? And wasn't it HUD's mandated sub-prime lending that broke the world in 2008? I can't believe it is even still here to cut.

Department of Defense needs a 50% trimming: how can it take 600,000 civilian employees to buy bullets and beans for 1.1 million uniformed troops, and why are we defending Germany? Back when it was called the War department, we all knew what it was supposed to be used for.

In a previous post, I laid out my proposal for converting the government pension system (social security) to a system of personal retirement savings accounts over a generation, and in another 2-part piece, laid out a comprehensive plan for real health care reform that phased out Medicare. Anyone who still talks about "saving" them clearly doesn't comprehend they are already broke.

TSA, NIH, FDA, EPA, SBA, INS, DEA – too many agencies, not enough space to list them all . If it has three initials or a czar running it, chances are it is 8 parts useless jobs program for unionized federal workers and 2 parts marginally useful function of government. I would make "scrap" the default setting unless someone can justify their existence who doesn't work there or get their grants from them.

Add them up, and we have just cut the size of the federal government in half, from 24% of GDP to 12%, and turned deficits into surpluses so the debt can be paid down and tax rates can be lowered. These are real and permanent cuts, not smoke and mirrors or single-year accounting gimmicks.

And government will not only be cheaper, it will be better. We will have better schools, more energy, real retirement security, health care that is better and more affordable, strong economic growth, more jobs, and higher wages. Think of it as a $1.7 trillion economic stimulus bill each and every year, only one that Jim Doyle can't get his hands on.

Think my cut list is too drastic? Look at it again, and tell me which one of these departments has fulfilled its promise. Tell me which you would even notice if no one told you it was gone. Tell me which one you are willing to pay 71% higher taxes to keep around – that's what it will take from all of us to keep all of the government we have now.

My campaign cards say "Tim, Not Tammy". You have seen my list; you should ask her to show you hers. We both claim to be against deficit spending: one of us (Tim) has shown you how we would stop it, and the other (Tammy) has voted for every penny of it.

Affirmative Action

You either believe that institutionalized racism is wrong or you don't. I happen to believe it is wrong, and therefore oppose Affirmative Action in any form.

To support Affirmative Action, you must first accept its prerequisite belief that people of color and women are inferior to white males. This is a vile and ignorant idea; one that people of conscience should vehemently reject.

In fact, I reject the whole notion of group rights and group responsibilities – we are not a flock of geese. I believe that each individual *person* has been endowed by their Creator with a unique set of talents and potentials, rights and responsibilities.

These rights preceded government. Governments are created to protect them, and governments are thrown off when they don't - this is the lesson of history.

Affirmative Action does not protect the equal rights of all persons; it diminishes the rights of some in order to bestow favors to others. It chooses its victims and beneficiaries on race and gender alone, not on merit. And it dehumanizes the very people it claims to be helping; forcing them to surrender their individuality and take up membership in a herd.

It assumes that Martin Luther King and Rodney King are cut from the same cloth; that Nancy Pelosi and Nancy Reagan are one. It is shameful that we fill our children's heads with such nonsense.

We teach the majority of them that they are not capable of individual achievement, that they are not good enough to compete with the minority of white boys. We teach them to wait for someone else to level a playing field, instead of learning to run uphill.

Politicians love to use that term – level playing field. As if life was a straight-line march across 100 yards of manicured lawn with white lines and referees and yard markers; where you get a reward every ten yards and everyone else stops a waits for your instant replay whenever you perceive a slight. Good luck with that.

Real life is a full speed off-road chase with no destination, no time clock, and no instant replay. It is the thrill of victory *and* it is the agony of defeat. Reaching the summit is only meaningful when you pick your peak and climb it yourself; taking a helicopter ride to the top only enriches the pilot.

The view from the top is the same for the climber and the rider; but they see vastly different things. And only one will be prepared to conquer the next peak, and the next, and the next. Affirmative Action turns climbers into riders; it enriches only its helicopter pilots, those who have made millions marketing victimhood.

Democrats would rather be race pimps than risk losing the votes it buys them, and Republicans are so PC they are afraid to call a spade a spade – in fact, I would bet that many of them just flinched reading that agricultural reference.

Libertarians are the Party of Principle - it is not difficult for us to see things clearly and speak plainly about them. Affirmative Action is bigotry encoded into law; it is immoral, unconstitutional, un-American, and it has deprived persons of *all* races and *both* genders from reaching their full individual potential.

50 years of Affirmative Action is enough. If it has worked, it should no longer be necessary; if it has failed, it should no longer be desirable. In either case, it should no longer be.

Afghanistan

The current debate over *how* to prosecute the war in Afghanistan sidesteps the more important question: *why* should we prosecute a war in Afghanistan?

Under our Constitution, only Congress declares a war, and the only the Executive carries it out. In this case, President Obama has declared Afghanistan a "war of necessity" and Congress is now running it by committee. 180 degrees wrong.

And why is Afghanistan a necessity? Eight years ago, ok, but this is now. Most knowledgeable analysts say we need to stay another decade to achieve our current military objectives, although they can not state clearly what they are. Some even speak of intergenerational occupation - at $35 billion per year and growing.

I can think of no compelling national interest that would justify continuing our military occupation in Afghanistan for another year, let alone another generation.

Afghanistan is simply not worth it. Its GDP is less than the budget *deficit* of California. It has nothing to trade, except heroin. It buffers Iran from Pakistan, two nations of even lesser importance to us economically. It will never be a useful military ally, unless we breed horses that can swim the oceans.

The argument that our leaving *might* allow terrorists to reconstitute there is not convincing; there are a dozen nations where they have already set up shop – should we go invade and occupy them all?

When we leave, the Afghans either will or will not go back to their violent notions of social justice. Whether that decision comes in two weeks or two generations will not change the outcome. The only question is how much we will spend and how long we will wait to discover their choice.

The Clinton administration showed us we can not treat terrorism as a criminal justice matter. The Bush administration showed us we can not confront it militarily. Terrorism is an intelligence matter; it requires an appropriate, if distasteful, level of counterterrorist direct action. Occupation is not the answer, and more troops longer do not change the question to make it so. The question is still – why?

We have done our good deed for the Afghan people – we toppled the Taliban, chased Al Qaeda out, and ended the brutal oppression of women and girls. That was eight years ago, and it only took our brilliant military only 6 weeks to accomplish that feat with a minimum of civilian casualties. That was the war in Afghanistan; the state of affairs that followed has no name. It is certainly not peace.

We should bring back our troops from Afghanistan.

And while we are at it, we should bring them home from Iraq, Kuwait, Japan, Germany, South Korea and the dozens of other countries who pay us nothing to provide for their defense while they compete against us in the global economy. We are the land of the free, not the land of the free mall cops.

We should maintain the force strength and technology to obliterate any nation foolish enough to attack us; that will insure they don't. It wasn't our good intentions that convinced Gadaffi to shut down the terrorist training camps in Libya, it was our good aim – one missile under the tent made us more secure than a decade of diplomacy did or a generation of occupation could ever hope to.

But military might is not foreign policy. Our only foreign policy imperative is free trade. It is also our best national security policy - customers and suppliers don't kill each other. Nations occupied feel no such self-restraint.

Age of Consent Is 18

It is wrong for the government to deny rights of seniors solely on the basis of their age; equally wrong for juniors, sophomores, and freshmen.

There is no principled reason to deny adults the right to choose for themselves whether to drink alcohol or not. This is a matter of personal preference and belief.

Rights aren't rationed out like some annuity over time; we were endowed with all of them at birth. They are held in trust for us by our parents or guardians until we reach the age of consent, and the age of consent is 18.

The federal government imposed a drinking ban on 18-20 years through an extortion scheme of the lowest kind in the 1980s. It required states to adopt a 21 year old drinking age or be cut off from federal highway funds. Age discrimination has been the policy of both the Democrats and the Republicans ever since.

Think for a moment what message this sends to our young adults. Their first interaction with their government as vested citizens is to have their rights taken away through an unconstitutional encroachment of the federal government over state sovereignty. Goodbye civics class; hello mob rule.

Liberty denied should not be the first consequence of citizenship. So this will be the first bill I introduce as Congressman from Wisconsin's 2nd District – the Universal Age of Consent bill.

Now, before the blissfully inebriated students in section O at Camp Randall break into chants of "Tim, Not Tammy", let me say this: don't think I am a champion of 18-year-old drinking, because I'm not. I am a champion of 18-year-old Liberty. Don't vote for me so you can drink; vote for me so you can choose for yourself how you will live.

And that is really what this all about; the idea that you don't have to ask permission to live. It is difficult to imagine now that we were once a nation that lived by that simple proposition. We were proudly independent; our demand of government was to be left alone, not to be taken care of. Our Declaration of Independence insisted upon the right of the individual to pursue happiness; not to be immunized from the consequences of our pursuits.

Libertarians believe that each of us has sole dominion over our persons and property, and that any voluntary exchange between individuals is just. We believe that any act of force or fraud that interferes with voluntary exchange is unjust, including prohibitions on adult alcohol purchases by the State.

Vote Libertarian. Vote for Tim, Not Tammy.

TOOTH FAIRY GOVERNMENT

Ba-Roke Obama

For a smart guy, President Obama sure seems to be having trouble understanding that we are broke.

Granted, it is difficult to comprehend our fiscal situation with billions and trillions being thrown around – numbers no person can comprehend. However, if we drop 8 zeros off all those big numbers, divide them all by 100 million, we can describe the federal budget in terms that every family can understand.

Drop the 8 zeros, and it goes like this: we make $27,000 a year, and we spend $42,000. Let's stop right there. 99.9% of us – those who *don't* have a Ph.D. in economics from Harvard – can see exactly what the problem is: we are spending 55% more than we have.

We have been living stupid for quite a few years now, so we already owe $120,000 on our Visa card. Stop again for a second. 99.9% of us – those who *don't* run the Federal Reserve – know that you can't carry debt that is 4 times your annual income.

This year we will borrow another $18,000 to pay ongoing government expenses, including interest on the outstanding balance. 95% of us – those who *didn't* take out a sub-prime loan at a place in a strip mall next to the Check 'N' Go – know that you have to pay back a loan.

And we spent the money we borrowed on some pretty dumb things. We borrowed $7,800 last winter for a stimulus bill that didn't stimulate anything. It was supposed to add 3 million new jobs; we lost 3 million. Now we had to borrow another $300 to pay for the extra unemployment benefits.

We borrowed $8,500 to give to some big banks last fall; now they want to give us $2,000 back and call it square.

We borrowed $500 to buy into GM and Chrysler then borrowed another $40 to give people to buy our cars. They took the money and bought Hondas instead; that really sucked. $1,200 for Iraq and Afghanistan wasn't enough, so we borrowed $300 to send more troops.

The Senate is busy trying to spend another $8,500 we don't have on health care; the House already passed a version that would cost $12,000 that we don't have.

Not to mention that we will need to come up with $60,000 in a few years to pay for our parents' retirements; we already raided the social security trust fund a long time ago. How do you do all that on $27,000 a year? Maybe rob a bank.....oh, wait, we own them now. Never mind.

And then out of the blue Hillary grabs a microphone in Copenhagen and promises all the poor countries we will give them $1,000 because the temperature might go up...or go down...or stay the same.

Ben Bernanke at the Fed had an idea: he took all the dollar bills out of our wallets, cut them in half and declared we had twice as much money now. So the banks could loan more to the government and charge more interest..to..themselves. Time Magazine gave him man of the year for that one.

Economist Stephen Moore gave me an even better idea this week, tongue in cheek; just take a sharpie and write a zero behind the number on each bill in your wallet. That way, we would all be 10 times richer, right? $1 turns into $10, $20 turns into $200; it's no different than what the Fed is doing, just a bit more obvious.

Let's get serious. The U.S. government is ba-roke, Barack – when are you going to get that? And I mean everyday Lindsay Lohan broke, not just-on-taxday Donald Trump broke.

I don't care what Hillary said in Copenhagen, you don't have any money to give; not $100 *billion*, not $100 *million*, not $100 *thousand*, not even $100. And we aren't giving you any more of ours; you are on your own.

BTU Bucks

Here is the idea of BTU-bucks; its really pretty simple, not the stuff of a Nobel prize....no wait, I take that back now that the bar has been lowered a tad.

The whole purpose of money is to be a surrogate for something of tangible value – it is the convenience of taking a coin to purchase an axe, not have to carry a pig all the way into town to barter. Markets can only regulate supply, demand, and price if the unit of measure is constant.

Imagine the chaos if the government strengthened and weakened the meter or stone. Would we be taller or lighter just because the government said so? Neither are we richer or poorer when currency is strengthened or weakend.

From 1779 to 1913, the value of the US dollar was constant largely because the Constitution prohibited the use of fiat money as legal tender; coins had to be minted from gold or silver, and certificates (paper dollars) had to be redeemable on demand for gold.

In 1913, the Federal Reserve system was created (unconstitutionally), and shortly after that the gold standard was abandoned. And our dollar is worth less than 1% today than it was more than a century – the century we did not have a central bank and we did have the gold standard.

So why not go back to gold? Well, there is $57 trillion of money in the world, and there is $17 trillion of gold, both denominated in US dollars. I have not seen a practical plan to deflate the world's currency like that without inviting the apocalypse.

And gold was merely the most convenient technology when money was invented; it has no special advantage today when nearly all of our money is just bits on a computer and a promise to pay embedded in metal strip on a plastic card.

So back to why we need money at all? Its only purpose is to facilitate exchange by providing a common measurement of value for things as different as pigs and software licenses. It is a surrogate for the things themselves.

How much money do we need? As much as the value of our economic exchanges; more than that causes inflation, less causes deflation and credit freeze. The value of anything is determined by supply and demand, money is no exception.

How do you measure the value of the economic transactions of billions of people around the world using different currencies to do billions of different things? Economists rely on after the fact statistical analysis to measure GDP; it is late, always requires an adjustment, and is easily manipulated by governments. The saying goes: "keep torturing the data until it confesses".

My idea (I'm sure I am not the first) is that the most reliable indicator of real economic activity – i.e. people making things, growing things, trading, educating, creating games to play on the phone - is the amount of energy that is consumed in doing so.

The world's economic activity is universally accepted as the driver of demand for energy. Inverted, that means that energy consumption is the most reliable measure of real economic activity. And consumption is measured daily, not estimated quarterly in retrospect.

California Dreamin'

If you want to view the prototype for Yes-We-Can America, you need look no further than California – farthest west, farthest left, and farthest in the tank.

Last year, California was the first state to reach the brink of default, with a $40 billion budget deficit, proportionately only slightly higher than Wisconsin's. It is no accident that California edged us out for the gold medal in fiscal insanity.

California was first to jump on every left-wing, big-government idea to come down the pike: stricter auto emissions, energy tax, drilling bans, tax and regulate business and industry out of their state, college education entitlement, smoking ban, free health care and welfare for non-citizens, bi-lingual, sub-prime loans, mandatory recycling, taxing the rich, and legislating through the courts.

California has doubled state and local government spending over the past nine years and now they can't pay for it. California also has among the highest rates of taxation on personal income, capital gains, and sales. It has the steepest angle of tax progression in the nation, with rates above 10% for top earners. Its tax burden per person is 6th highest among states.

Let's check the equation again: socialist agenda + tax the rich = broke.

Liberals in denial blame California's fiscal problems on the recession. Nice try, but their deficits were already at critical levels in 2005, when their economy was at its peak. This stuff does not even work in boom times.

A reasonable person would learn a lesson from California; a Democrat would make it his blueprint for the nation. President Obama's anti-growth economic, tax, and environmental initiatives mirror those that have brought California down. And here is Wisconsin we seem to be hell bent on catching them in the race to insolvency.

At least the rest of can see clearly where the nation is headed, so I guess we should thank California for proving that the laws of economics are not subject to amendment by legislators who never bothered to understand them.

When Californians were asked last year to increase their taxes to pay for their own government spending, they voted no. Congress, who apparently knows better than Californians, sent them $20 billion of your money instead.

Where did that money go? The city of Villejo pays its policemen $190,000 per year in salary and benefits, 90% of that when they retire at 50. California teachers earn 35% above the national average. A captain on the San Francisco Fire Department makes $250,000 – captain, not chief.

And having burned through its $20 billion handout in less than a year, California is preparing to come back and ask for more of your money this year. My answer is the same: sure, you can have all you want at $50 per barrel. Start drilling…dude.

It is more than a little annoying to be lectured about "sustainable development" from economic illiterates whose anti-energy agenda is clearly *unsustainable*. California has the mountains for hydro, vast open spaces for wind, and the sun shines on their solar panels every day.

They passed their own climate change bill in 2006. Where are all those green jobs? Where is the booming sustainable economy? Why do they have to buy electricity from coal-fired plants in Idaho? Idaho, let the record show, is not in default.

California was not struck by a horrendous natural disaster; it is a man-made disaster – socialism – that has taken them down. They were not harmed by global warming, the damage was inflicted by the global warming movement.

Look, if Californians want to have a fling with socialism, that's fine – the reason we have a Republic and a 10th amendment is so that states can govern themselves any way that they choose within the Constitutional framework.

What works can be repeated in other states, and what doesn't can be dumped without taking down the whole Republic. The key word there is "dumped" – not subsidized, copied, and rammed down the throat of the whole nation by executive order.

It is one thing to blunder over the edge of a cliff in the dark; it is quite another to follow a fool in broad daylight.

Channeling Enron

Ever wonder what happened to all the scummy-bears who did the creative accounting at Enron, Arthur Anderson, and WorldCom? I'm guessing they must have all gotten government jobs from the stimulus money.

Because politicians are not smart enough to think this stuff all up on their own.

If you recall, the House version of health care was scored by CBO in July at something over $1.2 trillion dollars. The director of CBO was called on the carpet for the treasonous acts of addition and subtraction.

On Wednesday, Speaker Pelosi announced she had a new Bill with an even more robust public option, and miraculously this new and improved ShamWoW of a Bill was scored by CBO at less than $850 billion! Did Jeff Skilling get paroled Tuesday? Does CBO outsource work to Leavenworth now?

We won't know how she managed to make the public option "more robust" while reducing its cost by 40%, because she wouldn't show us the CBO analysis. But she said she showed it to Senator Harry Reid, as if he were the Good Housekeeping seal.

When Harry wasn't busy checking Nancy's math for us, he was running his own Enron-esque shell game over in the Senate, trying to pass the first $257 billion of his own health care plan as a separate measure now, so the rest of it would stay under the $900 billion that President Obama said he would sign.

The Senate Bill started leaking oil when they got busted for keeping it under the $900 billion ceiling by cutting physicians pay 25% and then freezing their wages for 10 years. Obviously, these brick-heads forgot who wears the rubber gloves when it's bend-over time.

Michigan Senator Debbie Stabenow must have had the first appointment ("you might feel a little discomfort, Debbie"), because she rushed right back and introduced a bill to increase doctor's pay and unfreeze the freeze – but of course her separate bill would not count towards the $900 billion cap. I guess I can see how they think we are gullible enough to buy anything – after all we keep re-electing them.

Next we discover that those 10-year costs from CBO are totally bogus - counting 10 years of new taxes (yes, the T-word) and only 5 years of benefits. In order to make good on their baloney promise to keep health care reform deficit-neutral, they had to push most new benefits back to 2015 to make the numbers fit the lie. Kenny Boy Lay would be so proud.

This, by the way, is *exactly* what it was that Enron did to land everyone in jail - count multiple years of revenue and single years of expense to mask operating losses. The sub-prime mortgage pimps did the same thing, and apparently it is the only thing Congress learned from either scandal.

In business, we have an effective way of giving connivers, chiselers and serial half-truth tellers an opportunity to overcome their character defects. We fire them. And we don't pussyfoot around about it - it is a matter of survival, as corrupt organizations inevitably fail, and fail spectacularly.

Enron was a success story for free market capitalism, not an indictment of it. The market took care of Enron and their accomplice Arthur Anderson – they were purged with extreme prejudice.

The best part of the Enron story is that when they came to Washington for a bailout with the first "too big to fail" sob story, President Bush said no. The story had one happy ending at least – the perp-walk. Today, the government would have bought Enron; Barney Frank would be complaining about their bonuses in the daytime while Tim Geitner was paying them at night.

Call it "ethic cleansing" – it happens every single day in the private sector. But there is no such ethic cleansing in government. All those politicians and regulators who rigged the game in Enron's favor for a decade are still with us – only now they have seniority and run the joint.

The fools messed up energy, they messed up banking, they messed up housing, and now they have turned their sights on health care.

With a straight face, our Socialists continue to demand a public option to "keep the private system honest", even though they have lied, cheated, and cooked the books to try to shove it down our throat. And just who exactly will be running this new Department of Honesty – Congressman cash-in-the-freezer, or Senator wide-stance, or Governor taste-of-Argentina, or Secretary tax-cheat?

But no amount of accounting kitty litter can disguise the stupidity of plowing ahead with the dismantling of our health care system by people who either can't add and subtract or can't tell the truth. Or in the case of Congress, neither.

These guys can't run health care; they can't even run a little tiny fraction of health care. The government has had 6 months to prepare for H1N1 and it is still easier to get a Nobel Prize than a flu shot. In a rational world, that would be the end of it.

Chump Change

Peter Townshend said it more succinctly than anyone before or since: "meet the new boss; same as the old boss". And it's looking like we all got fooled again.

A lot of Obama voters must be feeling some buyers' remorse right about now, wondering how change we can believe in turned into chump change.

Let's start with the war. He has adopted George W. Bush's plan for withdrawal from Iraq, he is sending even more troops to Afghanistan, and he has expanded the war into Pakistan. He kept Bush's Defense secretary and top generals in place. He was going to bring the troops home, remember? Looks like the only thing that changed is his mind.

And he was going to close Guantanamo, which most people took to mean releasing the men being held there. Not so fast. He still intends to close Gitmo, but to hold the men somewhere else and continue the Bush/Cheney policies for enemy combatants. And we still don't ask and we still don't tell, and we haven't closed a single base overseas. That's our new commander-in-chief. Sure, he won't waterboard anyone, but they stopped that 6 years ago anyway.

Off the top of my head, I can't name a single foreign policy change of substance since Mr. Obama took over. Ok, we shot the pirates and sent Bill Clinton to retrieve 2 wayward journalists from North Korea, and he sent the other Clinton to Africa to rip into some poor kid who asked her a question. I don't think Condi Rice would have been so boorish, so maybe should count as a change.

Candidate Obama rightly took Bush's Republicans to task for running up the debt and tacking earmarked pork projects to unrelated legislation. President Obama is making W. look like an amateur, racking up more debt in one year than Bush did in 2 full terms.

Obama's stimulus plan was 100% porked-up earmarks, a new world record for gluttony at the public trough. And remember we were supposed to see all bills 5 days before they were voted on in Congress? What he meant was only the ones he thinks we will like.

He told us to wait until June to evaluate his economic plan. Unemployment was supposed to be lower, foreclosures were supposed to be lower; so were business failures, bank closures, crime rates, illegal immigration, interest rates, and bi-partisan rancor in Congress.

All of them went up, sorry. The only thing going down is the temperature, and that was supposed to be going up with all the carbon dioxide we are pumping into the atmosphere, remember? Damn those tea party wingnuts – they even screwed up global warming.

Obama hasn't just stuck with the Bush bailouts; he's doubled down – increasing the money for TARP, paying out bonuses at AIG and buying more banks. He re-appointed Bush's guy Bernanke at the Fed, and hasn't gone after any of the d-bags who caused the sub-prime mortgage mess that wiped out your 401(k) last year.

The President didn't just give more money to GM and Chrysler, he bought the companies. And then he gave people $4,500 to go buy a Hyundai. And they told us George W. Bush was the dumb president.

Meanwhile, the stuff that the Democrats really wanted – cap and trade, health care, and card check – are all stuck in Congress. Not that it is a bad thing, but they have enough votes to do whatever they want without the Republicans. How bad must these bills be if they can't even get Democrats to vote for them?

And how are those tax cuts working out for you? 95% of us were going to get one, remember that? Unless, of course, for those of us who smoke, buy things, sell things, or invest.
I hate to say I told you so, but I did. I won't rub it in, because I know that many of you who supported Obama feel betrayed and hurt already. I just want to insure that you learn a valuable lesson for the future – don't believe in tooth fairy government.

Mr. Obama promised all sorts of things he can't deliver. He is President, not King. The entrenched special interests that both parties depend on for campaign cash don't care who is in the White House; it's people like Nancy Pelosi, Dave Obey, and

TOOTH FAIRY GOVERNMENT

Tammy Baldwin that provide their return on investment, writing favors into the fine print of legislation that nobody reads.

Climatista!

In the movies, international leaders respond to looming environmental apocalypse by sending Bruce Willis into space. In Copenhagen, they send cash to Sudan.

Whatever you believe about the science of global warming, you can't possibly still think 20,000 European socialists can save us from it. Their solution is predictably lame: transfer wealth from rich countries to poor ones. Yawn.

Paying a $10 billion per year guilt tax to third world dictators will not cool the planet, but this has never been about science; it is simply the latest front in a century-long attack on American ideals of liberty and capitalism. We should quit pretending it is something else.

The Copenhagen Climatistas are not fighting to save the planet; they are fighting to hold on to an illusion of U.N. relevance in a world reconfigured without them by the ascendance of Asian capitalism.

In the past quarter century, billions of people have turned to American-inspired capitalism to raise themselves out of the poverty that the previous half a century of European-inspired socialism brought them. Rejected by thinking humans, the one-world statists have turned to rocks and shrubs to find a constituency for their discredited ideas.

President Obama should not go to Copenhagen. What is at stake there is American sovereignty. We are the richest nation because we are the most productive; and we are the most productive because we use the most energy. Energy equals prosperity, and should not give up 40% of ours just because a handful of collectivist dinosaurs find their impotence frustrating.

Energy is the currency of economic liberty. The goal of climate fascists is to seize control of it and ration it according to their own ambitions; to regulate the economic activity of the whole world. Democrats seek their approval; Republicans fear their scorn; Libertarians refuse to indulge them their world government fantasy.

TOOTH FAIRY GOVERNMENT

Our energy is not theirs to ration. Our prosperity is not theirs to negotiate. Our Liberty is not theirs to trade. Vote Libertarian. Vote Tim, Not Tammy.

RepubliCoke And DemoPepsi

Let's call them RepubliCoke and DemoPepsi; each have their loyal fans, but most us buy whatever brand of big-government cola is on sale.

We elect RepubliCokes when they promise us they are New Coke; tax cuts, balanced budgets, humble foreign policy, judicial restraint, local control, no earmarks, term limits – things like that.

But then they turn out to be RepubliCoke Classic; neo-cons and theo-cons and big government decepto-cons. So we fire the RepubliCokes and give DemoPepsi a shot when their marketing guys come along with a better pitch-man and a snappy slogan – "hope and change" comes to mind.

We think we ordered Diet DemoPepsi, but what comes in the can is the full-strength socialist stuff, and they hold us down on the ground and force it down our throats by the caseload.

Choking and drowning in the stuff, we cry "no more Pepsi!" (think Virginia, New Jersey, Massachusetts), but the RepubliCokes hear this as "mandate!", and assume we want *their* brand of big government cola shoved down our throats by the caseload.

Wrong. We don't want any more big-government cola shoved down our throats by the caseload – not RepubliCoke and not DemoPepsi.

That is the message of the Liberty movement, tax protests, town halls, Patriot groups, Tea Parties, the CPAC straw poll, the Massachusetts election, and the phenomenon of spontaneous citizen activism across the nation. The revolution is on, cola boys, and you are not invited.

That message is not new; it is just louder. It has been sent over and over again since 1968, the first in a long string of mostly lesser-of-two-evils elections between RepubliCokes and DemoPepsis where the winner's singular qualification for the job is that he isn't the other guy. 52/48 is not a mandate, it's a whim.

TOOTH FAIRY GOVERNMENT

Half of us don't even care enough about RepubliCoke or DemoPepsi to vote anymore. We drink whatever the waitress brings us, because it all tastes the same – wars, taxes, debt, special interests, earmarks, welfare, corporate subsidies, and some cola dweeb telling us what we can and can't do with our own stuff in our own homes.

That non-voting half of Americans has realized that the lesser of two evils is still evil; they will vote when there is something to vote for, not against. They want the Un-Cola, candidates who have minds of their own, who are not puppets of handlers and pitchmen whose only concern is taking back market share from the other Cola.

You shouldn't live your life constantly tethered to a big-government cola drip bag filled with *either* RepubliCoke or DemoPepsi. Shuffling through narrow halls with your head down and your gown open in back is undignified.

Quit shuffling. Ditch the drip bag. Grab an Un-Cola and live. Vote Libertarian.

Crap and Tirade

Before we roll over and take the cap-and-trade energy tax, it must be pointed out that this economic buzz-kill has not worked anywhere it has been tried.

Europe does cap-and-trade (this Europhile stuff is getting on my nerves) and its carbon emissions have grown over the past decade, about the same as ours has without cap-and-trade.

C&T is supposed to create a zillion new "green jobs" and spark a third industrial revolution, bringing forth a plethora of new products that sip energy. And what is the unemployment rate in Europe? And where are all the new products flooding in from across the Atlantic? I must have missed the all-electric Beemer.

Proponents of C&T justify it on the basis that it will bring down carbon emissions and save the planet. It does neither. The reduction in temperature that C&T advocates claim (their number, not mine) it will produce after 20 years is less than one half of one degree. I defy anyone to go stand outside and tell the difference from 76.2 and 76.5 degrees.

The economic damage we will inflict on ourselves (again their number, not mine) is 1% of GDP. Have we learned absolutely nothing over the past year? Each point drop in GDP is about 350,000 jobs. Maybe those of you who have recently lost yours could explain to government workers and teachers who have immunized themselves from reality why this is a bad thing.

Compounded over 20 years, reducing GDP growth by a point will cost us trillions of dollars. We could use this money to pay off some of the trillions of dollars of debt we have racked up instead of making our great-grandchildren pay it. Independent estimates have put the cost to the average household in increased energy costs due to C&T at $1,500 per year.

And for what? 4/10 of one degree. Maybe.

We tried a version of cap and tried about a dozen years ago – it was called Enron. They were trading energy tranches and derivatives (that term ring any bells, AIG investors) and it nearly bankrupted California. It took another decade for California to eco-bliss itself into bankruptcy, but they finally made it this year.

Ah, California – showing the way on environmental suicide. 6th in taxes, tops in welfare, toughest auto efficiency standards, toughest on industrial use, toughest zoning, first to ban smoking, banned mining, banned drilling, banned logging, ran off most of their industrial base years ago……… and now that they dug themselves into a $40 billion hole, they are expecting the rest of us to bail them out.

Sure, we'll give you $40 billion, Arnold – at $40 a barrel. Start drilling, dude.

The audacity of some people. Not only do they expect us to bail them out from the mess their loopy socialist fantasies have created, but they want to impose that nonsense on the rest of us.

You didn't learn a thing, Nancy. You guys had 40 years out there to show us the way; you screwed up the best state we had so stuff the attitude eat crow.

More Cap and Less Trade

No surprise that once again, Congress has it 180 degrees wrong. We don't use too much energy because we are rich; we are rich because we use a lot of energy. We need to use more – not less – and quit apologizing to the planet as if it had feelings.

Energy = prosperity. All you need to do is replace one word with the other to know what makes sense and what is folly. Why in the world would we want to cap your prosperity? Why should Al Gore and a few of his buddies get to trade your prosperity? Who decided to leave your prosperity buried in the ground?

Recently, I was in Peru and had the chance to observe some of the poorest and least productive farmers in the world; they work like dogs day and night to make about $500 a year. They don't use any energy; they dig in the dirt with hand tools. Not a smidgeon of greenhouse gas emitted, not even an ox fart.

North Dakota, on the other hand, has the richest and most productive farmers in the world; in fact, it has the most millionaires per thousand citizens anywhere. They are all about the tractors and combines and aerial crop spraying and trucks and trains to haul all the food to market. One North Dakota family can feed thousands of us and take the winter off down in Corpus Christi.

Do the farmers in North Dakota have Nancy Pelosi to thank for their prosperity? No, they have John Deere to thank for that; and John D. Rockefeller, and a hundred other greedy capitalists that did us the great favor of producing new things and not running for office.

And go check your pantry and see how much of your food that keeps you alive came from that Peruvian guy with the minimal carbon footprint we are all supposed to admire and emulate. He can't even feed his own family, let alone yours. You can thank those greedy capitalists, too.

Farmers are not unique; every human endeavor requires energy; and the more energy we use, the more productive we become. And productivity is all that will increase real wages. More energy = more prosperity. Less energy = less prosperity. Still like cap and trade? Then I can't help you, but thanks for making it this far.

Imagine what a gallon of gasoline would cost if we repealed all the taxes and regulations that limit supply and distribution? If we just let the people who knew what the hell they were doing build modern refineries and pipelines and compete for our business without the government telling them what and how much to produce and what to charge? Sure, they would get rich, but so would we; wouldn't that be fun? We already did this once in the 1980's so its not like I'm a genius or anything.

Here's my energy policy: NO CAPS and real TRADE - you trade 50 of your cents with the guy who owns Kwik Trip for a gallon of his gasoline. Everyone else stand down, except the guy who owns the Mobile station across the street who might offer to trade you *his* gasoline for 48 cents. Watch and learn, members of Congress, watch and learn.

Instead of the government spending our tax money to prevent our energy from getting to market, we should sell those reserves to people who will drill and mine that oil, gas, and coal like it would spoil if it stayed underground one more day. And we should drop all the subsidies of alternative fuels that are not economically viable – ethanol, solar, wind. And we should let people build nuclear power plants that want to; it is clean, safe, and affordable energy. And we should not tax energy anywhere along the supply chain. That is how we get gas for less than 50 cents.

Here's a bonus: available and affordable energy will produce available and affordable health care, food, housing, and education. Everything we do is done with energy, and the last thing we need to do is make those things even less affordable by raising energy costs. Do you expect the drug companies will honor that famous pledge to reduce drug prices by $80 billion after we increase their energy costs by $100 billion? Do you think there might be an escape clause down in the fine print, or do you think Joe Biden is smarter than 1,000 drug company lawyers and pulled one over on them?

Here's another bonus: when we use our own energy, there will be a glut of oil on the world market, and oil prices will plummet, taking down the cash flow that finances tin pot dictators and terrorists all over the world. Isn't it better to save our children from wars and terrorism than to save a ungrateful planet that was supposed to get warmer but refused to cooperate?

Here's another bonus: instead of having their accountants manipulate the book valuations of reserves and tax credits to invent profits on paper, the oil companies would only earn profits when they sold us something of value. We would choose which company makes money and which ones fail. They would have to please us, not the fundraisers for Congressional campaigns. Wouldn't that be nice?

Last year, when they wanted to bailout their buddies on Wall Street, our politicians kept telling us that credit was the "lifeblood" of our economy. It's not; energy is. Restricting the supply of energy (CAP) and increasing its cost (TRADE) is the dumbest thing yet in an era of incredibly dumb things that have brought our economy to its knees.

Dangerous Weapons

Last week, President Obama's attorney general said the administration would pass a new "assault weapon" ban. While Nancy Pelosi has said publicly she did not intend to take the measure up, she slipped it into the bill to give D.C. residents voting privileges, and Dianne Feinstein and others in the Senate have started the drumbeat for more gun bans.

So here we go, back through this whole 2nd Amendment slog again. The question of whether or not the right to own weapons is a constitutionally protected individual right has been argued, asked, and answered by the Supreme Court last year. That should have been the end of it. There has never been any question that the Constitution prohibits people living in the District of Columbia from voting.

Knowing this, Congress passed a law giving DC residents the vote and infringing on their right to bear arms; a twofer that perfectly illustrates why the 2nd Amendment issue is so critical to all citizens, not just gun owners.

The importance of gun rights in our political discourse is not the guns part, it's the rights part. A government that shows its contempt for the 2nd amendment will show no mercy when the 1st, 4th, 5th, or 10th inconvenience their agenda. They already have.

History shows us that a people become enslaved to the state one right at a time, so non-owners who sit this one out do so at their peril. Today, it's my guns; tomorrow, it's your books; the next day, it's your business. If anyone thinks this is paranoid delusion, let me remind you that government gave itself the power to terminate private medical treatment – adult abortion, I call it – in the "economic stimulus" bill.

The wording of the 2nd amendment is quite clear to me. If any question lingers for others, it is quickly answered by a cursory read of the contemporaneous writings of the founders. Samuel Adams wrote, "The Constitution shall never be construed ... to prevent the people of the United States who are peaceable citizens from keeping their own arms."

Can that be stated any clearer? No.

Congress is made up mostly of lawyers; they know precisely what "shall" and "never" and "infringed" mean. The phrase, "their own", is definitive about who is to decide what arms are kept.

There is no straight-faced argument to be made that a gun ban is Constitutional, so let's be clear-eyed about what Congress is preparing to do - violate their oaths and pass a law that is in direct conflict with perhaps the most explicit right guaranteed by our Constitution.

There is no right to choose in the Constitution, no right to privacy, no right to health care, education, affordable housing, clean air, or a job. The founders knew the importance of all these things, but did not give government the power to provide them. However, they saw fit to include an explicit right to keep and bear arms.

It is not grouped with other things as are many of the provisions in the bill of rights, and it was not left to the blanket coverage of the 10th.

The 2nd amendment is the exclamation point for the 1st. The 2nd is the guarantor of the other 9. They thought about it carefully for four years, and if the American people wish to amend the Constitution to remove the right to bear arms, it should be done via the prescribed process of Constitutional amendment, not through legislation.

Many of us can recite from memory the words from our Declaration of Independence, "We hold these truths to be self-evident, that all men are created equal, endowed by their Creator with certain unalienable rights, that among these are life, Liberty, and the pursuit of Happiness".

Fewer of us recall that that the sentence does not end there. It goes on to say, "that to secure these rights, Governments are instituted among men, deriving their just powers from the consent of the governed, that whatever any form of Government becomes destructive to those ends, it is the right of the people to abolish it, and institute a new Government".

I don't think that could be stated any clearer, either. How sad that our current leaders choose their words to intentionally deceive us – assault rifle, economic recovery, affordable housing, no child left behind, patriot act, to name just a few.

And don't send out the black Suburbans, Nancy – I'm not advocating the violent overthrow of the government. We don't need to do that, as the framers – far wiser than the current leaders - provided the means for us to overthrow our government every two years via the ballot box, and we should do exactly that in 2010.

I don't know what kind of weapons my neighbors own – they pose no threat to me. If God forbid I should ever need to call on them for assistance, I *hope* they have more firepower than the criminals I would need to be protected from if I had to call on them. In fact it will give me great comfort to know they have an arsenal.

The *really* dangerous weapons in this country go to work every day on Capitol Hill – there are 535 of them, and they scare me to death. A criminal might break into my house and steal my property, but it's done and over. My Congressman keeps coming back and taking more – more money, more liberty, more choice, and more opportunity. Most days, I don't feel the need for the protection of Congress; I feel the need to be protected *from* Congress.

The list of my most dangerous weapons includes my table saw, my snow blower, my garage door opener, the cheese grater, a chin up bar – all of which have sent me to the emergency room, so perhaps I should attach the inflammatory adjective "assault" to each of them, and lobby to have them banned. Sorry, but public safety trumps your right to grate cheese, and too bad for you bible-clinging grater-nuts out there.

My guns have never caused me or anyone else harm; that's more then I can say for myself. I must have gotten lucky and picked out some especially well-behaved ones.

When Congress passes their assault weapons ban and the leaders of our government line up in front of the cameras to heap praises upon themselves for their noble civic achievement, I hope that each of you will be haunted by these chilling words from the last century:

"This year will go down in history. For the first time, a civilized nation has full gun registration. Our streets will be safer, our police more efficient, and the world will follow our lead into the future!" – *Adolph Hitler [1935] The Weapons Act of Nazi Germany.*

Energy Choice

When the weatherman's prediction doesn't come true, we blame the weatherman; when the Global Warming guy's predictions don't come true, we blame the weather.

The central theory of Global Warming is that the burning of fossil fuels emits Green House Gasses (GHG) like CO_2 which are raising the earth's temperature. Well, that was the theory. Despite massive increases in CO2 emissions over the past decade, the earth has not warmed; in fact, it has cooled ever so slightly since 1998.

My position on Global Warming has been consistent since I first read about it 20 years ago – it is an interesting theory with no evidence yet to prove it.

The "proof" of Global Warming is not what you might think. It is a handful of computer models developed in the early 1990's that predict the earth will get warmer, and then predict all kinds of calamities that would result. Computer models. That's it. That's what this is all about.

The objective scientific evidence – temperature readings, earth's rotational speed, ocean levels, etc. tell a different story. None of what the computer models predicted has come true. The earth has not warmed, the seas have not risen, the rate of rotation has not changed. They should have by now, according to the computer models.

Stripped of the hysteria and self-interest, the Global Warming debate is simply whether you believe the computer modelers are infallible. It is a religious belief.

Our politicians tell us there is consensus in the scientific community; this is untrue. There is a deep division between those who forecast what might be and those who observe what is. More than 400 peer-reviewed articles have presented evidence that conflicts with Global Warming theory. More than 13,000 scientists have signed a petition stating that the theory of man-made Global Warming is not proven.

The important thing is not whether you believe in Global Warming; the crux of the matter is whether those who do have the right to impose their beliefs on those who don't. It is a classic Constitutional issue of the separation of Church and State.

There is no greater threat to your Liberty than the loss of energy choice. The government is about to mandate steep reductions in the use of fossil fuels, and there are no viable alternative energy sources to make up the BTUs that will be lost. We should quit listening to people who keep pretending there are. When we mandate a 50% reduction in carbon energy, we will require ourselves to use 50% less energy, and therefore accept a 50% reduction in our standard of living. Why? Computer models.

And to those who think its about time SUV drivers got their comeuppance, let me remind you what we use energy for. Heating nursing homes and air-conditioning hospitals; powering MRI machines and running incubators for premies; powering laboratories seeking cures for autism, cancer, and HIV; running the factories that process our food, clothing, drugs, household goods; getting us to and from work, and powering the factories, offices, mines, farms, warehouses, airports, schools, and government buildings that providing a place to work and earn a living; running our wastewater treatment plants and pumps to provide the water without which we would die; lighting our cities at night to prevent us from raping and killing each other. No energy, no life.

Maybe you think that giving up 50% of those things would be fine - I don't. Maybe you don't mind old people dying of heat stroke by the thousands when power is lost – I do. After 30 years and tens of billions in research and investment, renewable energy - wind, solar, hydro – make up only 7% of the energy we use to live. 85% comes from fossil fuels. The "clean and green" alternative to fossil fuels does not exist.

Biofuel? It would take 625,000 acres of corn to generate the same amount of BTU's each year as one 4 acre coal-fired power plant. Wind? The wind farm needed to light up New York City would be all of Connecticut – all of it. Solar? Let's just move on to nuclear. I am a proponent of nuclear power; if it were up to me, I would build hundreds of nuclear plants – enough to supply all of our electricity without one gram of particulate pollution. And then use gasified coal to run our cars and trucks and small engine; we have 200 years of the stuff. Cleaner air, energy independence, have a nice life Hugo Chavez, Saudi princies, and

TOOTH FAIRY GOVERNMENT

oil rascals everywhere. But people are too scared of nuclear, thanks to that stupid Jane Fonda movie.

Civil Rights activist Roy Innes has rightfully described access to energy as the most important civil rights issue of our time. Economic development and personal income are dependent on affordable and reliable energy. The heavy equipment operator can only earn 5 times the shovel hand's wage because of the additional work his bulldozer can do with the energy it uses. Income is directly tied to productivity, and productivity is directly tied to energy.

You have a right to use as much energy as you choose. No one has the right to deny you that choice, regardless of how fervently they hold to their beliefs.

EU – Say It Like It Is Written

For years now we have had to endure the incessant lusting of our American socialists after all things European; as it turns out, EU is not just an acronym, but also the correct pronunciation – eeewwww

We should not take pleasure at the suffering of others, but there is a delicious irony in watching the smug and condescending bureaucrats of Europe plunged into a financial crisis of their own making. The Obamalosi crowd rubs our noses into the Keynesian doo-doo, holding up Europe as the poster kid for good government and public morality.

They love Europe, with its government health care, cap and trade, nationalized industries, central banks, unions, fat pensions, VAT taxes, summers off, high speed rail, international law, 2-hour lunches, climate change, punishing tax rates, regulations and commissions galore, deficit spending, Nobel prizes, and gun bans.

Well now you can add economic default to the list of splendid European accomplishments. After decades of living large on their welfare-state spending spree, Greece, Portugal, Spain, and the U.K are now on the brink of default with a handful of other countries not far behind. They will have to get bailed out by the barely-stronger EU zone nations – just as Wisconsin had to bail out California because they were goofier than us.

Like any good bender, everybody is your friend when you're running up the tab; it's the paying part that is lonely and hurts your head. We feel your pain, Greece.

If you care about the economic future of our own great nation, watch the EU meltdown closely over the coming weeks, months, and years. This is what waits at the end of the trail we are marching foolishly down.

And take note that our U.S. federal budget deficits are the same as Greece as a percentage of GDP - they just have a 20 year head start on us in accumulating debt at a suicidal rate. But we are rapidly catching up; another 10-15 years and we will be right there. Watch Greece; the ghost of economics future.

TOOTH FAIRY GOVERNMENT

There is nothing to envy about Europe. Don't wear a speed-o, don't stop bathing, don't hold the fork in your left hand, or ride a bike with a basket (unless you like to ride a bike with a basket), and for heaven's sake don't elect liberal democrats who are economic illiterates. That is how they got into this mess.

Rebel against Europe and everything it stands for. See your dentist, buy a gun, ride a Harley, shave off that chin mullet, send the zip-up turtleneck to Goodwill, and ditch those skinny glasses with the wide colored temples. I don't have a firm position on techno – pro-choice, I guess.

We have moved way beyond the old paradigm of left-right in American politics; the choice is now up or down, more government or less, a return to free market capitalism or continuation down the road to democratic socialism, European style.

Rarely does a future course of action reveal itself so plainly as it has in the Euro-zone financial crisis; we can't say we have not been warned.

Don't Stop At Health Care

The problem isn't that advocates of government health care compare American life expectancies to those in Europe. The problem is the comparisons stop there; they don't tell you the rest of the story.

Per capita income is 29% lower in Europe than in the U.S., and payroll taxes in EU-15 nations are 30%, twice the 15% rate we pay. Thus, the average take home pay is 43% lower in Europe than here.

Would you take a 43% pay cut for life just to spend an additional 1.6 years in a nursing home?

Americans consumers spend $9,700 more per household than their European counterparts. We have more appliances, computers, cars, and electronic devices per household; as a result, we spend less time on domestic chores than Europeans, and have more leisure time.

How do you define living: 2 extra years of cleaning your floors by hand, or a lifetime of riding jet skis and snowmobiles on weekends?

The size of the average home in EU-15 nations is less than 1,000 square feet, compared to 1,875 in the United States. The poorest Americans average over 1,200.

No wonder they put up with long waits in doctors' offices; there is more room.

In 2006, unemployment in the EU-15 was 8%, compared to 4.7% in the United States. Worse than that, 42% of Europe's unemployed stayed that way for 12 months or longer, compared to only 12% of the unemployed here in America.

Another reason to wait for care: no job to go to.

In the United States, women hold 45% of decision-making positions in business and industry. In Sweden, the socialist nirvana, the number is only 27% and it goes downhill from there to Italy at 18%. As it turns out, capitalist women fare much better than their socialist sisters.

TOOTH FAIRY GOVERNMENT

Ouch! How do you say "women's work" in Italian?

Economic growth over the past two decades has been 50% higher in the United States than in EU-15. Since 1980, the United States economy has created 57 million net new jobs; the European Union has created only 4 million, most of those in government.

I could go on and on, but I believe I have made my point. It is a simple one, really: Europe sucks. America is better, so quit trying to ruin it, Tammy.

Vote Libertarian. Vote for Tim, Not Tammy.

Fairtax

There are only two ways to fund government; tax today's citizens, or steal the money form tomorrow's. It is a choice between the injurious and the immoral.

How much government we should have is a different question than how we should pay for it. The existing tax code is designed to punish and reward particular behaviors; it is a maze of preferences, subsidies, loopholes, and differential rates that no one understands and nearly everyone finds ways to evade.

Taxes discourage the thing that is taxed. We increase the cigarette tax to discourage smoking, liquor taxes to discourage drinking, gasoline tax to discourage driving and so on. Conversely, we reduce taxes to incentivize things like charity, home ownership, education, and business relocation.

Our existing tax system discourages work, savings, investment, profits, and job creation in the United States. It rewards sloth, overconsumption, debt, and job transfers abroad. We use the tax code to punish wealth and achievement, and then wonder why we have less of them.

I support the Fairtax. For those who may not be familiar with it, you can learn about it and its advantages at www.fairtax.org. Fairtax is endorsed by 80 prominent economists, including a Nobel Prize winner. It is supported by 82 current Congressmen and Senators.

Fairtax is an initiative to abolish the IRS, eliminate all existing forms of federal taxes, and replace them with one single tax on consumption – a sales tax that would be imbedded into the price of everything we buy. People who earn below the poverty line would be exempted by means of a prebate.

Fairtax is not perfect, and it is not an ideal Libertarian solution for taxation, but it is a light-year improvement over the system we have now, and it has a realistic possibility to become law. There are several reasons Fairtax is better, but I want to point out the two I think are most significant.

I can't think of a more effective way to reduce the power of the federal government than to take away its power to dispense favors and punishments though the tax system. Fairtax does that, and should be enthusiastically supported for that reason alone.

The special interests that corrupt Washington receive the returns on their investments through preferential treatment in the tax code; both the Democrats and Republicans play this game. Take away the power to grant favors, and there is no reason to lobby for them. The best campaign finance reform possible is Fairtax.

And it is the best economic stimulus possible. It is estimated that we spend $400 billion each year in tax compliance costs. That is money diverted from productive investments that create jobs and increase incomes. Fairtax also levels the playing field for U.S. goods sold abroad and foreign goods sold here, removing the current tax advantages of goods produced abroad.

The United States has the highest corporate taxes in the world. Investment capital is being driven out of this country and jobs leave with it. Adopting Fairtax would turn that around, and the United Sates would attract foreign investment again, and add the jobs that come with it. Fairtax = More Jobs.

Tammy Baldwin opposes Fairtax. She prefers the tax code as it is, where her friends can be rewarded and her enemies punished; where you pay more than your fair share so others can pay less than theirs.

Foreign Policy

A rational U.S. foreign policy only has three parts: 1) we will buy your stuff, 2) we will sell you our stuff, and 3) if you attack us we will obliterate you.

Our only vital national interest is free trade - unfettered, unrestricted, unregulated, unencumbered, full-throttle capitalist trade. Bring it.

We should immediately withdraw from every single trade agreement to which we are a party. A legitimate free trade agreement is a blank sheet of paper; any addition of black ink sets the terms and conditions under which governments restrict the rights of individuals to exchange private property. That is both unwise and un-American.

And besides, governments don't trade, people and corporations do. My company does deals in Mexico and Canada – I'm quite sure that neither we nor our trading partners have ever read NAFTA. It has no relevance, other than to present some bureaucratic barriers and paperwork to be dealt with after-the-fact.

We should lift all sanctions, tariffs, embargoes, duties and restrictions on the flow of goods, services, labor, intellectual property and capital across our borders. We should allow our citizens and companies to trade freely with anyone in the world, while taking care to protect copyrights, patents, trademarks, national security secrets, and contract sanctity.

Free trade is the key to pulling ourselves out of this recession and insuring strong economic growth for decades to come. It is also our most formidable security guarantee; a trader does not kill his customers, he needs them to survive and prosper.

And we should also immediately suspend all forms of foreign aid. "You got something to sell? No? See ya." It is not right to tax Americans to provide unearned benefits to citizens of other countries. Worse yet is to tax Americans to prop up the corrupt regimes in other countries that could not stand alone without our aid. Foreign aid breeds perpetual dependency and hinders economic development; it insures poor nations stay that way forever.

Nations whose only access to American capital is through exchange of goods will quickly develop their resources and learn to make things that people want to buy. We raised ourselves up out of poverty 200 years ago through free trade; the Chinese are doing it now. There is no reason the poor nations of Africa, South Asia, the Middle East, and Latin America can't be next. But they must first be weaned from the teat of foreign aid.

Quick – name 3 accomplishments of the United Nations in the past 40 years. I rest my case. And right behind it should go the IMF, the World Bank, NATO, the OAS, WTO, and every other bogus international organization to which we have ceded sovereignty over the past century. These organizations have accomplished nothing, other than to provide a lavish lifestyle to the legion of bureaucrats who live large at our expense and mock our values.

We need a strong military to defend trade routes from foreign disruption and piracy. But there is no compelling reason for us to maintain permanent military bases in dozens of foreign countries, or to engage in military interventions that are not legally sanctioned by a Congressional declaration of war. Not since World War II has Congress done its most solemn duty.

Our military personnel are citizens, too; it is not right to ask them to risk their lives for a cause for which their elected Representative will not even risk a vote. And our warriors should not be tasked with social work in foreign lands; that is a waste of their courage, their training, their skills and commitment as war fighters. Fighting wars is their only purpose; we should be grateful they are willing and we should not squander their valor on fool's errands and meaningless adventures.

We should maintain an overwhelming military capability that is rarely, if ever, used. Basing our military assets on our own soil increases our safety and security, it does not diminish it. Who do you think Hugo Chavez fears more, the 82nd Airborne units fixing potholes in Afghanistan, or the units at Fort Bragg rested and ready to respond in a heartbeat should he do something incredibly stupid?

Some will argue that mine is an isolationist foreign policy that will encourage rogue states like North Korea and Iran to do insane things like develop nuclear weapons in secret and threaten their neighbors. What is their second best argument?

And why is it our problem if they do? North Korea may someday attack South Korea and there could be war on the Korean peninsula – that would be tragic for both peoples. But if we have no troops based there, why does that become *our* war? No conflict need become our war unless and until our sovereign territory is attacked.

And Part 3 of my foreign policy is obliteration if attacked – certain and swift. We now take great pains to reassure nations we would not use nuclear weapons if provoked. Bad move; we should make it expressly clear that any first strike on U.S. property will result in a retaliatory strike that will insure complete annihilation of the government foolish enough to have instigated it. Whether that is nuclear or conventional is our choice, not the initiator of force.

We should not eschew the nuclear option, we should *guarantee* it. This is not a traditional Libertarian position on national defense, but it is defensible. It is certainly saner than the shared policy of the Republocrats over the past 50 years – permanent garrison occupation of most nations of the world and a series of undeclared invasions extending into perpetuity that have cost millions of lives and trillions of dollars.

This three-part policy is not isolationist. It expands our engagement with the entire world - on equal terms as friendly trading partners. Nations who would insist on letting their ideologies deprive them of the economic benefits of trade could do so at their own peril. Of what consequence is that to us?

And finally, this common-sense foreign policy would oblige the nations of Europe to pay for their own defense, rather than have us pick up their tab while they give themselves free health care and summers off.

TOOTH FAIRY GOVERNMENT

Get Your Shovels Ready

As soon as I heard the President utter the phrase "shovel ready" last winter, I knew the title of this week's blog post. I knew the hardest part would be deciding which outrageous use of "economic stimulus" money to write about. We have a winner.

As you may recall, the American Recovery and Reinvestment Act (ARRA) was supposed to fund infrastructure projects that were approved and planned, just waiting for funding. This is the story of one such "infrastructure project" right here in Wisconsin.

The project that was proposed and approved for ARRA funding was an expansion of the existing Youth Apprenticeship Program in North Central Wisconsin. The Youth Apprenticeship Program prepared students who were willing to study and work by providing apprenticeships at local employers while they were still in school.

Students benefited by learning valuable and relevant job skills. Employers benefited by having a pool of trained workers to hire from upon graduation. My company's Rhinelander plant facility participated in this very successful program, and we have hired many graduates of local high schools or technical colleges who have apprenticed with us in the trades.

The biggest problem with this program is that there are not enough jobs available in local industries to provide on-site work experience for all the students enrolled. Employers are not reimbursed for the cost of OJT training and can only absorb a few students at any one time. With the economic downturn, many employers could no longer afford to take on apprentices at all.

A group of local civic leaders wrote up an application for ARRA funds to expand this Youth Apprenticeship Program by providing reimbursement to local employers for some of the costs of providing on-the-job training for program participants. This would eliminate the "waiting list" for current students to fulfill their OJT requirements, and expand the number of students enrolled.

The expansion of the Youth Apprenticeship Project made Governor Doyle's wish list, and was approved and funded through ARRA. What was implemented, however, bears no resemblance to what was proposed, approved, and funded.

The State of Wisconsin gave implementation authority for this "shovel ready" project to the North Central Wisconsin Workforce Development Board (WDB), a 9-county consortium of state, county, and local agencies. The North Central WDB didn't use the ARRA funds to expand the Youth Apprenticeship Program; instead, it developed its own new government-run job training program. And then it set out to manufacture some needy students. So much for "shovel ready".

According to the North Central WDB Plan supplement, it will market to "low-income, displaced, and underskilled adults and disconnected older youth." Its recruiting partners are "various media sources, schools, high risk and alternative education programs, W2 area providers, social services providers…….community shoppers, additional community and faith based community organizations, and OSO partners."

And who are the recruiting partners recruiting? The Plan states "out of school youth and at most risk of dropping out; youth in and aging out of foster care; youth offenders and those at risk of court involvement; homeless and runaway youth; children of incarcerated parents." The Plan emphasizes "outreach to Native American organizations and County Probation and Parole".

If this doesn't sound like the Youth Apprentice Program, it is not. This is a welfare program, run by the welfare industry, for the benefit of the welfare industry. It is as blatant a misappropriation of government funds as you will ever see. Appropriate money for student apprentices, then give it to government hacks.

The purpose of this program is not to help youth or employers. It is to increase the number of state and local government welfare industry workers. The agencies that make up the North Central WDB will add 120 government jobs with the funds hijacked from the Youth Apprenticeship Program grant and other ARRA earmarks.

That is more new government jobs than the number of youth (104) that are being recruited for job training, mostly for summer employment. According to the WDB class schedule, candidates will graduate from summer job readiness training August 14. I am losing count of how many ways this is stupid.

And what about that existing pipeline of Youth Apprenticeship Program participants the earmark was intended for? They don't qualify. What about the participating employers? Out. God forbid we would have kids who want to work learn about employment from employers.

Those Youth Apprenticeship kids showed some initiative and drive; they chose to work and study and make something of themselves. Employers who take in these young apprentices showed what *real* compassion is all about – we are helping those kids learn what it takes to succeed, not filling their heads with useless propaganda.

In the real world, if you can't contribute value in excess of your compensation, you don't have a job. The Youth Apprentice Program students learn how to contribute value and compete. I bet those poor summer school kids won't; there is no one to teach them. They will probably learn how to bank sick days, file harassment complaints, game the civil service exam, and count down the days to early retirement without a calculator. It is so sad.

So get your shovel ready, fellow citizens - this is just the first of many loads of crap coming down the pike under the false pretense of infrastructure investment. But we only have to take it until November of 2010; then we can vote the bums out and start over.

Government We Don't Need

Candidates love to pay lip service to limited government, but duck for cover when asked to name the specific federal departments, agencies, and programs that they would cut. I'm not scared; here's my list.

Start with Department of Education – abolish it. Nationalizing education dropped us to 17th in reading and 18th in math. Local control of schools and school choice will get us back to #1 in the world again.

Abolish the IRS and repeal the 16th Amendment. Replace our insane tax systems with a single national consumption tax – the Fairtax – that would save us $400 billion in compliance cost, and take away the mechanism for political corruption, our tax code.

Before there was a Department of Energy, we had plenty of it and it was cheap. Abolish it, and we will be self-sufficient again in two years.

Goodbye, Department of Agriculture. We need to dismantle the corporate welfare programs administered by the Ag Department. Farmers have the internet.

The Department of Labor is chasing jobs out of this country faster than the Department of Commerce can schedule trade junkets to the countries where the jobs went to. Abolish them both and keep jobs here.

Department of Interior? How would you even know that it isn't already shut down? We only have it because the government owns $6 trillion of land it shouldn't. Sell the land and pay down the debt.

Department of Housing and Urban Development. I think one global financial meltdown from government meddling in the housing markets is enough this century, don't you? Our urban centers will never develop until the government leaves them.

Bureau of Indian Affairs. Who is in greater need of subsidy, the folks playing the machines in Ho Chunk Casino in Wisconsin Dells, or the folks emptying them?

TOOTH FAIRY GOVERNMENT

End the Fed. Congress has the Constitutional authority to maintain a stable currency; there is no place for an unelected, unsupervised, and unaudited Federal Reserve System run for the benefit of a few giant banks.

DEA and Federal Prisons. Our federal drug laws are all side effect and no cure. We have not changed abuse or addiction rates one iota, and have added intractable new problems of gangs, crime, violence, and destruction of the minority families to the manageable social scourge of addiction. Hundreds of billions wasted for nothing.

Office of U.S. Trade Representative. What does the Government trade? People trade, companies trade, governments don't. Get out of the way.

Close overseas military bases and bring our troops home. Our government has a duty to defend us, not Japan, Germany, South Korea, Iraq, Afghanistan, and dozens of other countries most of us could not find on a map.

While we are at it, we need to gut the DoD civilian workforce. There are 600,000 civilians to buy things for 1.1 million warriors in uniform. That is pathetic.

Abolish the Department of Homeland Security. Homeland security is what Department of Defense is for.

Department of Health and Human Services. Replace social welfare with charitable choice; a dollar for dollar tax credit for charitable giving. It would double the funding for worthwhile charities, and eliminate the need for this bloated mess.

Mission to the United Nations. Quick, name three accomplishments of the U.N. - I know, neither can I. Let them scold us on their own nickel.

Repeal Health Care Reform. Whatever they pass, repeal it before it gets started.

Social Security, Part I: Tax choice at 65. When people reach 65, give them the choice to either continue to work – 100% TAX FREE – or to retire and collect social security and medicare benefits. Many people would choose to keep working and keep 100% of their earnings, reducing the stress on the Social

Security and Medicare systems, and keeping valuable knowledge in the workforce.

Part II – transition to personal savings accounts for both pensions and health care over 25 years. This would provide benefits to seniors to whom they were promised, but would allow young people to build wealth and retire with 4 times the income than the current system promises and will fail to deliver.

How's that? 75% less government spending, stronger Defense, more charity, better schools, more energy, no deficits, no bailouts, more jobs, and you gain more control over your life while you keep what you earn. That's my plan.

Can you beat it, Tammy? Chad? Peter? You send me your plans and I'll post them right here for everyone to read and comment on.

TOOTH FAIRY GOVERNMENT

Grow Up

To anyone who I may have offended by my choice of words in these campaign blog posts over the past year, may I say with all sincerity....grow up.

We all learned that "sticks and stones may break my bones but words can never hurt me" when we were about six years old; so if don't get that, you must be five.

And frankly, most of us are tired of letting you five-year-olds run our country.

That's right – I just called you five-year-olds. Go ahead and throw your tantrum now. Hold your breath and cross your arms, stomp your feet and get all indignant. It's what you do.

95% of us have to walk around on eggshells because a few of you prickly PC gerbils might pick today to go off your medication and get all traumatized by a word you don't like – a *word*.

Well here are too of them: get bent.

Hate Speech

The socialists have finally given us a definition of hate speech we can use: they hate it when we speak.

Before the ink was dry on the health care bill, liberals were already on the name-calling offensive, describing anyone who opposed their socialist agenda as racists, homophobes, white supremacists, fascists, or domestic terrorists.

I have yet to hear a single voice in the Liberty movement call for violence or for the overthrow of the government by force. I can't recall hearing a single racist remark at any of the political events that I have been invited to attend. Have you?

Last week the FBI added "sovereign citizens" to their list of hate groups in a bulletin sent to local law enforcement around the nation. Imagine that: it is now considered hateful to believe in the first principle of the Constitution – individual sovereignty. The media buried that story in the back pages, if they reported it at all.

It is a sad state of affairs when the defense of Liberty is considered hate speech; when belief in the Constitution puts you on a government watch list. It's a good thing government is incompetent, or we would be in grave danger.

Personally, I think the most vile and dangerous form of hate speech is when a self-appointed elite claim to know better than us what is good for us. It places their contempt for us and their hatred for our values on full display.

They are telling us that we are too stupid to decide for ourselves what is good, that we are incapable of attaining goodness independently from them, and that we can't be trusted to think and act of our own volition. That is some hateful stuff.

And who is it that is hurling hateful epithets upon black libertarians and conservatives, especially those who dare to speak at "tea party" events? They are cheered by the so-called angry white mobs; it is the liberal left-wing bloggers that call them "oreo", "uncle tom", and "spray paint nigger". And yet the media reports it just the opposite; tea partiers are the racists and liberals the victims.

TOOTH FAIRY GOVERNMENT

The hatred directed at black libertarians and conservatives is not about race; it is about success. The socialists hate it when *anyone* excels without their permission, but especially minorities and women who must be kept dependent upon the state for the socialist left to remain in power. They can not tolerate the sight of a black man or woman who has made it on their own; it exposes the lie.

That's what this hate-speech fuss is all about - keeping the socialists in power.

Democrats get hysterical when we call them by their rightful names – liberals or socialists as the case may be. I myself have been called a racist for simply using the term "socialist" in my speeches and writings.

One journalist recently went so far as to make up a racist quote, attribute it to me, and then criticize me for the message in *his* words – I guess he could not find anything suitably hateful in anything that I have *actually* said or written.

My comment correcting his fabrication was immediately deleted from his online article; and my complaint to his publication was returned undeliverable. That is the state of free speech and journalistic integrity on the left these days.

It is not hate speech to call me a libertarian; that is what I am. And it is not hate speech to call a socialist a socialist; that is what they are. The difference is that I am a member of the Libertarian Party; we actually named ourselves after what we stand for, while socialists hide from their proper name. On the political spectrum, we are polar opposites.

We oppose socialism because it is dehumanizing, and its legacy is war and genocide. When the economic policies of the socialist philosophy fail – which they inevitably do – regimes must use force to retain power of the people they have impoverished. Over 100 million were killed in the 20th century at the hands of the socialists. To this day, the left will not own up to that - they are the ultimate holocaust deniers.

Look back at the last 100 years of our own American history. Who took us to war? Wilson, Roosevelt, Truman, Johnson, Clinton, two Bushes – five liberal democrats and two liberal republicans. Seven big spenders who expanded the size and reach of government. Not one of them ran for office promising war; that came later.

It is ironic that our socialists call anyone who opposes them "Nazis". The German National Socialist Party came to power promising hope and change and economic recovery. Its first initiatives were gun control, health care, minimum wage, taxing industrialists, nationalizing energy, and demonizing the banks and insurance companies. Does that sound vaguely familiar?

If you think it could not happen here, you are wrong. It is happening here right now; the power of the state is being expanded daily and liberty is being diminished daily. President Obama has expanded the very wars he ran against; into Pakistan, Yemen, and likely soon into Iran. Where is the tipping point of socialism? Why on earth would we want to find out? Each step toward the brink is a bad move.

It is not hate speech to stand up against hateful things; it is hate speech to remain silent in the face of hateful things. And socialism is a very hateful thing.

Heads And Tails

Economic Liberty and personal Liberty are two sides of the same coin; you can not pretend to keep heads when you throw tails away.

While I have devoted a great deal of time in these posts to matters of economic Liberty - jobs, taxes, energy, health care, monetary policy, fiscal policy, and trade – it is personal Liberty that is the defining American virtue and the greater loss when the coin is stolen from us.

You have heard me say it many times: Liberty is the absence of government in choice, and Government is the absence of Liberty in choice. In Liberty, your choices are governed by your own conscience and beliefs; in government, choices are made for you by others. It is our choices that define us as persons.

Volition – the capability to form moral choices and act upon them - is what separates us from the beasts. Constraint of volition by force or fraud is inherently de-humanizing; it does not matter whether the constraint is imposed by individuals, corporations, or government, it is wrong.

A principled belief in personal Liberty is quite simply stated: government has no legitimate authority to regulate private personal behavior - period. It only becomes complicated when exceptions are made and we attempt to explain the contradictions that arise.

Too many of us demand Liberty for ourselves, while insisting that it be denied to others. We demand that government leave us alone in matters of keen interest to us, while insisting that government prevent others from doing things we don't like. We demand freedom from coercion while insisting that others be coerced.

None of us has the right to impose our values and beliefs on another against his/her will. As a practical matter, criminalizing private behavior doesn't get us less bad behavior anyway, just more criminals. Victimless crimes do not exist in reality; only in bad laws. Laws which are selectively enforced, prosecuted, and sentenced.

Most of us want government to protect our rights; not to protect us *from* our rights. As long as our choices do not infringe on the equal rights of others, we should be free to live as we see fit, not to live under the yoke of mob rule.

Libertarians, as our name implies, hold Liberty as our first principle. Our strict allegiance to *both* heads and tails of the Liberty coin is what separates us from modern-day Conservatives and modern-day Liberals, who choose their favorite side when it serves their purposes and disregard the other when it becomes inconvenient.

Absolutism in Liberty means, by necessity, that we must tolerate all sorts of personal behaviors and choices that we do not condone, endorse, or approve of. Annoyance is a trivial price to pay in order to live free.

In my generation, tolerance was taught as a virtue. We were raised to "mind our own business", to "live and let live", to "judge not, lest ye be judged". In political terms, the virtue of tolerance is embodied in a position of neutrality on social issues.

When it comes to the social issues - abortion, drugs, welfare, guns, religion, lifestyle choices - the proper role of the federal government is to keep its Interstate bridges in good repair. Head down, eyes closed, mouth shut – leave all that stuff to communities and states as the 10th amendment instructs.

Whether you choose to work three jobs, pray all day, or take drugs and curl up on the floor, you will be sufficiently rewarded – with prosperity, piety, or addiction - to self-regulate. There is no real need for the government to add its own punishments to the consequences of your choices.

Our Creator endowed each of us with Free Will, a gift so precious it was withheld from the angels. If HE did not deny it to us, who are we to deny it to one another?

Health Care Town Hall Speech

Why are we all wee-weed up about health care?

Because our politicians are forcing us to take sides in a contest between insurance companies and government bureaucrats. If that were a death match, most of us would be secretly hoping for a tie.

They are making this way more complicated than it needs to be.

Two years ago, I was wheeled in to Aspirus Hospital in Wausau, Wisconsin, paralyzed on my left side from the waist down. One day later, a team of neurosurgeons operated, 5 days later I walked out of the hospital, and a week later I was back at work. It cost less than my wife's car.

That's what is right about health care in America.

It took 6 more months to get the billing squared away and everybody paid. That's what's *wrong* with Health Care in America.

If our elected representatives were here today to listen I would tell them this: leave the first part alone, fix the second part, and then take the rest of the year off before you screw it up again.

We pay $2.6 trillion for health care annually in this country. It would take 95% of all taxes collected for the government to provide health care to everyone. Only $1.4 trillion of that has anything to do with making you healthy or keeping you that way.

The rest goes to the accountants, lawyers, social workers, billing clerks, government drones, jockeys, bureaucrats, actuaries, consultants, hedge fund mangers, claims processors, and benefits specialists – all those nice folks who *don't* wear rubber gloves when they bend us over.

Here are two changes that Congress could write in one page and pass in a day that would cut out most of that wasted 40%. 1) Indemnify providers against lawsuits in which there is no criminal negligence alleged, and 2) eliminate 3rd party payer by using Health Savings Accounts to pay providers directly. That takes two of the biggest snouts out of the trough.

If we had American health care at 40% less cost, they would be having angry town hall meetings in France. And that should be the goal of health care reform, to get the French all wee-weed up.

President Obama promised my employees they could still choose private insurance if we had a public option. Sadly it won't be up to either of them. The House Bill levies a payroll tax of 8% on employers who don't provide health care benefits. That is less than half of the cost of a decent insurance premium; it is a simple business decision to drop coverage and pay the tax.

Businesses don't have the luxury of dealing with the government that is promised, we must confront the one that is practiced. Don't blame the players when the refs change the rules.

We all know what improves quality, reduces cost, and expands selection – choice and competition. Markets don't work perfectly, but they work – we can't say the same for government interventions. What keeps the small town auto mechanic honest? It's not the policeman *or* the priest – it's the second auto mechanic.

We are supposed to like government health care because the Europeans live longer. I frankly don't care how old they are in Belgium. I would rather live free for 79 years than be a slave for 81. What about you?

Individualism

Does the individual exist to benefit society, or does society exist to benefit the individual? Libertarians are individualists. Liberty is our first principle.

We believe in individual rights, individual responsibilities, private property, and equality of opportunity – every person and contract is treated equally under the law. We believe in individual sovereignty – we set rules for government.

That is what sets Libertarians apart from Democrats and Republicans and many of the other third parties; they believe in group rights, group responsibilities, public property, and equality of outcome – that is achieving outcomes through unequal application of laws. They believe it is the proper role of government to set rules for us, and to decide what "public good".

Government and Liberty are opposing principles. In Liberty, your choices are governed by your own conscience and beliefs. In Government, choices are made for you according to the beliefs of others. Liberty is the absence of government in choice. Government is the absence of Liberty in choice.

Democrats are willing to risk Liberty to achieve social justice. Republicans are willing to risk Liberty to achieve moral order. Libertarians are willing to risk both social justice and moral order to preserve Liberty.

Libertarians believe that any initiation of force of fraud is unjust, whether done by an individual or by government. We believe that any voluntary transaction between individuals is just, and interference by third parties is unjust.

Remember FLIP: Free Trade, Limited Government, Individual Liberty, and Private Property.

We believe in a Constitutional government; that is limiting federal government powers to those explicitly granted in Article I section 8, and prohibiting government action in areas where authority is not granted to them.

We oppose foreign military interventions abroad, except for wars declared by Congress, and we oppose economic interventions at home, except for anti-trust enforcement and regulation of interstate commerce as required in the Constitution. We oppose laws that create victimless crimes – laws that ban voluntary exchange.

I believe that all of the founding fathers would have been Libertarians. They would not recognize the government we have now. Their governments spent less than 5% of GDP while ours approaches 60%.

The Libertarian Party was founded in 1971 and is the third largest political party in the United States. Libertarians serve in elected office in all 50 states.

We have been described as economic conservatives and social liberals; I would probably say social neutrals, as we believe the government should stay out of social and cultural issues altogether.

TOOTH FAIRY GOVERNMENT

Identity Theft Alert

Attention readers! Someone with access to your social security number has run up an unauthorized $36,000 debt on your account and is charging an additional $454 each month. The thief is the U.S. Congress.

Those are the real numbers – the per-person debt and deficit obligations that our Representatives are inflicting upon us against our will. We agreed to give them $6,000 per person in federal taxes to run the government this year; they are stealing an additional $5,500.

That is what the budget deficit is – the amount of government spending you didn't agree to pay for. This year, government plans to spend 71% more than we gave it. What would you do to your kids if they went to the mall each month and charged up 71% more than what you make? That is, what would you have done before they made it illegal to be a parent?

Politicians and media pundits make budget issues incomprehensible. Fortunately, there is a Dept. of Treasury website that publishes federal government receipts and outlays monthly: http://www.fms.treas.gov/mts/index.html.

Just money in and money out; no spin, doublespeak, accounting gimmicks, or shine jobs. Divide by 330 million to get your per capita share. Easier than a checkbook.

While per capita numbers help us comprehend government spending, they are a bit misleading. Babies are "capitas", but they aren't paying; neither are people who don't work, or who work for the government – they are on the spending side of the ledger. All of the wealth that is consumed by government spending is produced by people who work in the private sector – all of it.

There are roughly 110 million private sector jobs, so we can triple the per-capita figures to get a per-job perspective on spending. The current debt is over $100,000 per job. That debt is increasing at an average rate of $1,362 per month.

Working couple? You owe over $200,000 and your debt is going up $2,700 each month. Imagine the kind of home you could buy with $200,000 down and $2,700 per month mortgage payment. Or pay off your credit cards, or buy better health insurance, or pay for college, or take vacations, or give to charity, or invest, or care for family members in trouble, or send your kids to private schools – whatever you choose to do with an additional $32,400 each year.

College students? The President's budget *doubles* the national debt in 10 years. That is if his plans work perfectly, and they never do. You will owe over $200,000 per job; $400,000 for a working couple. If you were putting that $2,700 per month into an investment account and didn't have to pay back $400,000 of debt racked up by your parents and grandparents, you could retire young and live like royalty instead of getting royally screwed and working 'til you drop. You need to start paying attention to this stuff.

So let me ask you this, dear reader: if the choice was yours, would you send that extra $2,700 per month to Congress or would you use it for something else?

The choice *is* yours - you can vote Libertarian in 2010.

Who Pays?

If the world were a caring contest, even I might be a socialist. But the world is not a caring contest; it is a paying contest. Caring doesn't feed a hungry child – only paying does.

There are 105 million Americans who work in the private sector; we produce every penny of the $14 trillion of wealth that is created in this country. There are another 220 million people who live very, very well because we do what we do.

Too many of them think it is their job to tell us what we should do with the money we have earned. Mostly they think we should give more of it to them. That way they can care more while we pay. How nice for them.

Liberals and socialists are all about caring with someone else's money.

Tax returns of liberal icons Al Gore, Barack Obama, and Joe Biden, all three quick to chide us about our responsibilities to each other, have shown them to be dreadfully stingy when it comes to their own charitable giving. And for a party that claims its moral authority by caring with your taxes, Democrats sure seem to have great difficultly paying theirs.

If your only objective is to feel better about yourself, then seeking praise for making other people do things is close enough to count as an achievement. If you have spent your whole life renting self-esteem on someone else's tab, then accomplishment becomes conflated with intent, and caring does equal helping in your delusional mind.

I am quite proud of my son – he feeds hungry children. He does that by driving a semi truck, delivering bread from the factory to distribution points around the Midwest. Every day, he gets up in the middle of the night and goes to work. He feeds more hungry children than all the elected officials at all levels of Government put together.

I am also quite proud of my daughter-in-law – she clothes needy women. She does that by managing a clothing store. Every day, she stays late into the evening so that people who work during the day can shop for what they need. She has put more clothes on the backs of more people than all those politicians put together, too.

They don't work that hard because they care, although they are both caring people; they work that hard to earn a living. They don't expect you to pay their way, and they both worked two jobs when they needed to, rather than ask you to pay for the things they wanted to buy.

And so do all the people who grow the wheat, make the flour, bake the bread, stock the shelves, and ring up the cash registers. So do all the people who design, make, ship, label, stock, and tell you that your butt doesn't look too big in that dress. That is how people get clothed and fed in this country, not buy politicians blubbering on about how much they care.

Unemployment is not just a statistic; every job lost moves one person out of the ranks of those who produce, and over to the ranks of those dependent on those who still do.

TOOTH FAIRY GOVERNMENT

Immigration Reform

We have seen this movie before: Congress is rushing to vote an unread bludgeon of an immigration reform bill that does nothing to reform immigration.

This is getting predictable, tedious and boring. Neither party has had an original thought on the immigration issue in decades – the Republicans would send the National Guard to the border, while the Democrats would send Rev. Al Sharpton to Phoenix.

It is easy to criticize Arizona's decision to enforce federal immigration law when you don't live in Arizona. Libertarians are conflicted: property rights and personal safety need to be protected - indeed that is the first and only rightful purpose of government. On the other hand, we oppose restrictions on the free flow of labor across borders.

But this dilemma is not addressed by the false choice between amnesty and deportation; neither approach will solve the problem off illegal immigration. That will only be solved by making immigration legal.

The reason we have millions of illegal immigrants in this country is that the process to admit them legally is totally broken down. *That* is the problem that needs to be fixed – that is why people come here illegally. No one wants to talk about it.

It can take several years to get a visa to come here work legally; the system is full of quotas, loopholes, preferences, restrictions, corruption, and at the end of the day, decisions are arbitrary, political, and irrational. You would not accept a seven year wait to get a driver's license, you would drive illegally.

Labor is like any other over-regulated market - prohibitions and quotas create black markets and criminal enterprise whose effects on the community are much worse than the underlying free market effects the government originally sought to dampen.

In an unregulated labor market, where it would be easy to immigrate and emigrate legally, people would come and work for a while, save some money, *and then go home*. The inflow and outflow of labor would be managed by supply and demand, not by armed criminal gangs.

Labor moves around the world every day; Americans are up in the Oil Sands of Alberta, setting up factories in China, running banks, building roads and bridges, mining coal, teaching in Universities all over the world – we work there for a while and then we come home. We are not unique – transactional labor is commonplace.

It is ridiculous that 3rd world countries can figure out how to admit, welcome, and track temporary workers routinely while our own U.S. government continues to dork it up year after year, decade after decade.

While we have made it nearly impossible to come here and work legally, we offer generous welfare benefits to people who come here illegally and *don't* work. And our minimum wage laws drive the illegal immigrants and business owners into a criminal underground economy. Lastly, our drug laws add violence and gangs into the mix.

None of these are immigration problems; they are the consequences of welfare, economic interventionism, and prohibition policies.

These ill-advised government programs are not only attracting undesirables from abroad, they are producing home-grown undesirables in far larger numbers. They should be dismantled for the good of citizens and non-citizens alike.

Securing the border does nothing to alleviate the perverse incentives that welfare, tax, economic, prohibition, and our newly minted health care entitlement policies create. And amnesty for those here now will only encourage more to come tomorrow.

Immigration is a good thing, and open borders are a good thing. We are a nation built upon the character, drive, and idealism of people from all over the world who came here to work, to own property, to start a business, to live in Liberty. We need many more of them, and we need many less of the deadbeats who come to get a better handout than the one they would get at home.

The only real solution to illegal immigration is to make labor migration legal, to dismantle the welfare state magnet for undesirables, and then to let free markets manage the flow of documented workers across borders.

In Exchange For What

There are three ways to get what you want: you can a) exchange for it, b) steal it, or c) beg for it. One is morally defensible; the other two are government.

Government confiscates the earnings of productive individuals, then divvies out the spoils to those who have the most skilled lobbyists begging for them. Political Science majors will spend 4 years learning how to call it something else.

The confiscation comes in two forms: taxation of earnings, and devaluation of currency. Congress takes as much as it wants (fiscal policy), and then the Federal Reserve makes what you have left worthless (monetary policy).

The begging also comes in two forms: to gain unearned benefits for your self (social justice) or to force someone else to stop doing things you don't like (public good).

The two establishment parties differ at the margins over who to take it from, who to give it to, and who to punish; but both Democrats and Republicans embrace the steal/beg/punish model of big government. The machinery itself doesn't offend them; they just want to be the ones pulling the levers.

Libertarians are different; we reject the model; we want to dismantle the machinery. We think stealing is wrong, and begging is de-humanizing.

We believe that individual rights are inviolate. We believe your only entitlement is the pursuit of happiness; no one should deny it to you, and no one is obligated to buy it for you. It's not complicated.

This year, the federal government will confiscate $2.4 trillion of your current earnings and another $1.4 trillion of your future earnings (deficit) so it can spend $3.8 trillion of your money. In round numbers, that is $12,000 per person, $48,000 per family of four.

As Dagny Taggert famously said in the novel, *Atlas Shrugged*: in exchange for what?

TOOTH FAIRY GOVERNMENT

Less than 13% of it, about $480 billion, goes for the things that we authorized the government to do in the Constitution (Article I, Section 8). That's only about $1,500 apiece; freedom is not expensive.

That leaves the other 87% of federal spending going for things that are either extra-constitutional or flat out unconstitutional. Those cost us about $10,500 apiece; socialism is *very* expensive, a luxury good.

Imagine for a moment that taxes worked that way: only the first 13% were mandatory, and that the other 87% were voluntary. That family of four has $42,200 left over, so what does the government offer in exchange?

Would you invest in social security or would you choose a personal savings account instead? Would you purchase private health insurance or pick Medicare knowing it was just a few years from insolvency?

What are you willing to pay to defend Afghanistan, Japan, South Korea, Germany, the Balkans, Iraq, and 100 other nations into perpetuity? How much for the UN, WTO, IMF, World Bank, and foreign aid payments to regimes around the world?

Would you send your money to Department of Education or to your local schools? Private schools maybe, since you have $42,000 to spend as you see fit.

Would you rather fund the Department of Energy or use that money to buy some? Ditto the Agriculture Department? Go down the list: Commerce, Labor, HUD, Transportation, HHS, NASA, DEA, INS, ATF – well, maybe ATF if they *gave* us alcohol, tobacco and firearms.

You get the point. If we had a choice, there wouldn't be very much government, would there? We wouldn't buy all those other things with our own money, would we?

Well, it *IS* our money; and we *DO* have a choice. That choice is Tim, Not Tammy.

Like it says on my campaign website - I want to be your Congressman, not your mommy. I am not going to Washington to bring home the bacon; I am going there to shut down the slaughterhouse.

Which would you rather have – all that extra government telling you what you can't do, or the $10,500 you are paying for it? The choice is yours; I'm just running to make sure you have one.

Independence Day

The important divide in American civic life is not between Right and Left on the horizontal axis; it is between Up and Down on the vertical – do we want more or less government?

Where we each place ourselves on this vertical scale depends largely upon our understanding of the relationship between the individual and society. Does society exist for the benefit of its individual members (the individualist's orientation)? Or do individuals exist for the benefit of their society (the socialist's)? It is not an irrelevant abstraction; the answer shapes our view of the world and the role of government in our lives.

Government is the organized use of force to constrain action. To the individualist, it is the state itself which needs to be constrained. To the socialist, it is the individual. These are incompatible philosophies. One can only be advanced if the other retreats. This is the dimension of civic life measured on the vertical axis.

Today's Republicans and Democrats are both socialists, in that they seek to restrain the individual to benefit of society. They differ only on the purposes to which they would turn the power of the state against its citizens. They push and pull to the right and left against each other along the horizontal axis, but when given control of the levers of government, they have both pushed the vertical up with equal gusto.

In broad terms, Democrats constrain economic liberty to achieve their notion of social justice, while Republicans constrain personal liberty to achieve their notion of moral order. Whenever state power constrains its individual citizens, Liberty is lost; whether it is the Left or Right hand doing the taking is of secondary concern.

Libertarians do not seek to restrain individuals; we seek to restrain the state from taking our liberties. Economic liberty and personal liberty are two sides of the same coin; it is foolish to think we could give up heads and somehow retain tails.

It is the relentless assault on our liberties – from *both* the Right and the Left - that explains the increasing disaffection of the public for its government, regardless of which of the two major parties claims temporary custody of it. Most Americans don't want *either* the Right or the Left to lord over us. We see plainly that it is the unchecked power of the state that produces abject failures on *both* the Right (Iraq) and the Left (California).

There is an alternative to Right/Left; it is *Down* – a smaller, less powerful, and less intrusive government whose aim is neutrality, not ideology.

If one believes – as Libertarians do – that society exists to benefit its individual members, then it follows that the power of the state must be constrained to preserve individual sovereignty. The idea of individual sovereignty and limited government is not new, although it is once again considered radical. It is the noble ideal upon which our nation was founded. The holiday we are about to celebrate on July 4th is Independence Day; it is not Entitlements Day.

This nation did not just magically appear one day in 1776. There were over *two centuries* of American history before the Declaration of Independence; before the Revolution, our Government was organized on the premise that individuals exist to benefit the society to which they are assigned at birth. Government constrained its individual citizens and sought to impose its own notion of social justice and moral order upon them.

The state and its ruling elite claimed dominion over the natural rights of its citizens. The government claimed jurisdiction over private property. The state intervened in commerce to reward allies and punish opponents. A distant central government imposed mandates upon local governments and individuals, extracted exorbitant taxes and fees, and burdened citizens with public debts. Prosperity was not earned through merit; it was allocated by the state to those best able to petition for favors and pay for advantage. Sound familiar?

Human nature did not change on July 4, 1776. What was changed was the nature, size, scope, and purpose of our government. Two centuries of collectivism was rejected, and individualism was embraced. While the same diversity of views on social justice and moral order existed in their time as ours, our founding fathers had the wisdom to constrain the government to neutrality on these matters. They considered all possible directions for the new government; they rejected left and right and wisely chose "Down".

What followed was a century unlike any that had been brought forth before or since. These United States rose from a backwater colony to become the most powerful and most prosperous nation on earth. By 1900 – in just 10 short decades - Americans made up 3% of the world's population, yet produced 50% of its products. We abolished slavery, we rapidly increased life expectancy, we institutionalized private charity, and we led an industrial revolution that created the world's first middle class – a majority of citizens living in prosperity that had never been achieved before in all the great civilizations of history. Not the Byzantines, Persians, Romans, Egyptians, Greeks, Mayans, Ottomans, or any of the great dynasties in China.

It was not by accident that we became the most prosperous, the freest, and the most virtuous people on earth; our commitment to Liberty guaranteed it would happen. Neither is it by accident that in our recent decades we have become less prosperous, less free, and less virtuous. We have rejected the ideal of individualism, and our failure to constrain our government has enabled it to constrain us. We have exchanged Liberty for Government; we have traded Independence for Entitlement; we have surrendered Sovereignty for Subsidy. As a result, we are a nation in decline, and we have chosen our ruinous path ourselves.

It need not be. Americans changed our government once to install Liberty as its First Principle – this is the first Revolution that we remember each July 4th. We can do it again; and we must. We cannot allow future generations of Americans to be born into slavery – and make no mistake that we are becoming slaves to the State.

This time, our revolution will not be fought with bullets and blood; it will be fought with ballots and blogs. The weapons will be different, but the mission is not; restoring our individual sovereignty from a government who has denied it to us.

What is the purpose of winning independence from one government, only to become dependent on another? How do we honor the millions who fought and died to secure our Liberty by trading it away? What good is emancipation from one master if it is simply traded for enslavement to another?

This Independence Day, let us not forget what it is that we are celebrating - it is our independence from government.

Happy Independence Day.

TOOTH FAIRY GOVERNMENT

Irreconcilable Differences

The mommy and daddy of the nanny state filed for divorce Sunday night – all that's left now is to convince the kids the other parent is to blame.

Our year-long forced march into socialized medicine has sharpened the line of demarcation in this nation. On one side is the State and its dependent wards; on the other, freepersons who seek to make their own way in the world.

The former no longer countenance the independence of the latter, and the latter will not willingly live under the yoke of the former. We should quit pretending we want to live together any longer.

President Obama is correct on this point: the time for talking is over. There is nothing to further to discuss. It is pointless to pretend that Collectivism and Individualism can co-exist. There can be no dialogue between the looter and the looted.

People who believe it is their right to confiscate their neighbors' earnings and compel them to work for their benefit have already turned a deaf ear to reason, the law, the Constitution, the Ten Commandments, and the cries of their neighbor. What else can we say to them?

Back when government was limited, the Constitution served as a buffer between the State and the People, and legislative compromise was possible. If we have learned nothing else from this past month, it is that government is no longer limited.

Still need proof? The clincher was federalizing all student loans at the 11th hour by appending it to the health care Bill. Using kids with leukemia as human shields for such a brazen power grab is well south of shameless. The Department of Education will be the 7th largest bank in the nation, and will determine who goes to which school. We spent a good portion of the last century fighting nations who did this.

Health care, education, banking, autos, energy – the list of American industries nationalized in the past year would make Hugo Chavez blush.

But this is not Venezuela; our socialists are bolder. Liberal Democrats were reported to be "giddy" last week at the prospect of taking another $1 trillion from those who earned it. Watch any riot on the news – those looters are always giddy, too.

To all my giddy liberal Democrat friends, I would remind you that it takes just one election to turn all these new State powers over to Sarah Palin or someone you may find even more distasteful. It will serve you right.

And to all my outraged Republican friends, I would remind you that it was your party that appeased our socialists for decades and expanded the State yourself when you had the chance. By the time you decided to be the Party Of No, the party was over. Save up a bit of that righteous indignation for the mirror.

Libertarians take no joy in saying "I told you so." But we have warned you that this day was coming for 40 years. We have stood firm against each encroachment on your liberties, whether it came from the left or the right. You called us whacky, losers, paranoid, conspiracy nuts – how do you like us now?

The vote is over; the Health Care Bill is law. It will not stop children from getting sick; it can not compel miracles. The laws of supply and demand can not be amended through reconciliation. Its first visible consequence will be the hiring of 16,000 new IRS agents; they will not be taking your child's temperature.

As a result of Sunday's vote on Health Care, the government is vastly more powerful this week than it was last week. But the people who run it are no wiser and no more capable. That will soon become abundantly clear.

TOOTH FAIRY GOVERNMENT

Keeping Us Honest

Democrats insist on including a government option in the health care bill to "keep the insurance companies honest". That is an amusing thought.

The whole premise of government health care is dishonest. Does anyone actually believe that covering more people and improving quality will cost less? Do you think the government could give free steak and lobster to every hungry American and that would somehow reduce the national food bill? It doesn't work with CT scans either.

The true objective of health care "reform" that is being bandied about in Congress is to force the nation into a universal government-run system. For those who still doubt this, I ask you to consider the proposed 8% payroll tax that will be levied on employers who do not provide health insurance benefits.

The median private sector wage is $40,000, so an 8% tax is $260 per month per employee. A typical insurance premium costs employers somewhere around $800-$1,000 per month. It does not take a Ph.D. in Business Administration to figure this out: most employers will drop their 20% health insurance benefit and pay the 8% tax. It would be foolish not to, and fools go out of business – excepting of course fools who get bailouts from other fools in government.

So when, not if, our employers drop our insurance, we will all go onto the government plan. Which, of course, has been Tammy Baldwin's goal all along – universal, single-payer, government-run health care. Nancy and Tammy will blame evil corporations for dropping health insurance while taking credit for saving your children from disease and death. Like killing the husband, stealing the wife, and taking credit for saving a widow from starvation.

So when all that remains is the government option – let's call it Katrina Kare - then who will keep the government honest? Congressman cash-in-freezer? Senator wide-stance? Governor Argentina-on-the-side? Secretary of oops-I-forgot-to-pay-my-taxes-again? I can think of many places I would go for advice on honesty, integrity, ethics, and morality - the government would not be one of them.

Every resident of a small town understands that it is not the priest, mayor, cop, or mother that keeps the auto mechanic honest; *it is the second auto mechanic.*

It wasn't a "government option" that made Walgreens drop its generic prescription drug prices to $4, it was Walmart. In fact, the government option will *increase* drug prices as both Walmart and Walgreens will have to roll that new 8% payroll tax into the cost of your drugs. I guess we all must be rich, because we are going to pay every penny of that tax.

The answer for rising health care costs is more choice and more competition, not a universal government-run system. The Republican alternative is not much better than the Democrats – making the incomprehensible tax code even more incomprehensible with health care tax credits and deductions that none of us understand. In Congress, compromise means finding a way to benefit both trial lawyers and tax lawyers, so let's hope for gridlock.

Libertarians want you to make your own health care choices - not government bureaucrats, not insurance companies, not HMO's, not employers, not tax accountants, not trial lawyers, not hospital investors, not hedge funds, and certainly not members of Congress. Not Tim, and not Tammy - You.

We want to reduce the already overbearing regulatory burden that fixes prices, subsidizes bad practice, forces unnecessary procedures, prohibits alternative medicines, and drowns the system in mountains of paperwork that have absolutely nothing to do with making you healthy.

Members of Congress will be back in their states and districts in August. Ask them about that 8% payroll tax – if they wanted you to keep your private insurance, why put in an incentive for employers to drop it? Ask them if the government will sell you prescription drugs for less than $4? Ask them why they are taking away your health insurance but leaving malpractice insurance for the trial lawyers to feast on?

TOOTH FAIRY GOVERNMENT

Killing Our Golden Geese

In Aesop's fable, it was not the goose that was golden; it was the eggs that she laid. The wealth that was coveted was *produced* by someone of unique ability.

When the goose was killed, production stopped and the farmer was impoverished. Children understand the moral of the story, but apparently it is too difficult for socialists to grasp. They are stubbornly committed to killing our geese – the people who produce things and make us prosperous.

In January of 2007, Nancy Pelosi took control of Congress. Unemployment was below 4%, inflation hovered around 2%, and the Dow was at 14,000. Her agenda was blatantly anti-capitalist and anti-American.

She promised to tax the rich, to ration energy, to unionize industry, to destroy private health care, to restrict free trade, to seize excess profits, to confiscate capital gains, to regulate economic activity, and expand government. She delivered.

And over the next two years, the Dow dropped 50%, destroying 17 trillion of private wealth and gutting the 401(k) of ordinary Americans. 7 million people have lost their jobs, while several million more have seen their wages or benefits cut. Millions of homes have gone to foreclosure; tens of millions have lost value.

Tens of thousands of businesses have failed; thousands more have moved their operations overseas. The unemployment rate now exceeds 10%, and the U6 rate – unemployed and underemployed is just under 20%. The producer price increase rose last month at an annual inflation rate of 12%.

Much to Nancy's chagrin, the very rich are still very rich. Her socialist beat down has ruined the lives of average Americans. That should come as no surprise, since it was the average American who benefited *most* from free market capitalism.

According to the Bureau of Labor Statistics, we now have only 18.6 million people producing things - that is the total employment in manufacturing and construction *combined*. By contrast, government employment has risen to over 22 million.

Our economy can not recover when our barren hens outnumber our golden geese.

We have taxed, regulated, and unionized our golden geese to death. In 2010, we will kill a few more of them by raising taxes on income, capital gains, repatriated profits, and inheritance.

And then we will kill some more when we levy fines on businesses that do not provide health insurance. And then we will kill some more with cap and trade energy taxes. And then we will kill some more with Card Check – government-imposed unionization of a firm without an election.

If there are any geese left, we will get them with energy rationing once the socialists in Copenhagen tell the socialists in Washington how much energy we have been apportioned and how much payola we have to send to Africa.

But capitalists aren't geese; they don't wait around to be killed by ignorant socialists. They are taking flight and landing in places like Brazil, Russia, India, China, Vietnam, Columbia, Taiwan; I see them everywhere when I travel overseas.

I wish they were here; we need their unique abilities, talent, and drive here. It is the capitalists who made this country great; and it is the capitalists who are making other nations great.

Rights, Laws, and Victimless Crimes

The concept is simple: you do not have a right to anything that someone else must produce. Forcing someone to produce something for your benefit is called slavery.

You have no right to health care, housing, food, a specific job or wage, or the whole gamut of things that someone else must produce. You have a right to purchase those things if you choose, and you have a right to sell them if you choose. That's it.

In recent times, we have perverted the term "rights" to include all manner of needs, wants, desires, and covets. We have spawned a whole industry of advocates, activists, litigators, bureaucrats, victims, and pimps who make their living demanding and then enforcing faux rights created out of thin air.

Natural rights are those that you exercise yourself – speech, religious expression, association, property lawfully acquired, dominion over your person, self-defense. These rights are not fabricated by mortals; they are an endowment from our Creator – self-evident, as the Declaration properly states. Our Constitution explicitly prohibits government from infringing on our natural rights; in fact, that is its sole purpose.

And equal rights means equal – exactly the same for every single person who has reached the age of consent. Not more for some, or less for some. You don't get bonus rights for belonging to one group, and you don't get less rights for belong to another. You have all of your rights at birth, held in trust until you are a citizen at age 18 - 18, not 21.

Laws are different. Laws don't add rights; they confer privileges. Laws don't take away rights; they can only make it a crime for you to exercise them. Laws change; rights do not. Laws are fickle, responding to the shifting political winds of the moment; rights are universal and eternal. Democrats and Republicans have lost sight of the difference between rights and laws; Libertarians have not.

Just laws criminalize behavior that deprives a person of their natural rights through force or fraud. In the case of victimless crimes, it is the law itself that deprives individuals of their rights.

Libertarians oppose laws creating victimless crimes on principle – these laws are unjust.

Who is the victim when a 19 year old woman drinks a glass of wine? Whose rights have been denied when a cancer patient smokes marijuana to relieve his pain and suffering? Or a college professor who simply prefers pot to Vodka? What right has been taken from Bobby when Suzie safely carries a gun in her purse for protection? If person A agrees to work for person B for a specific wage, how has C been harmed?

No victim, no crime – a simple enough concept. It's not just about vices – it is about the whole range of human interactions. Libertarians believe that any voluntary exchange is just, and use of force or fraud to compel or deny exchange is unjust.

Victimless crime laws turn today's choices into tomorrow's felonies. Our prisons are full of people whose only offense is possession of a plant that my grandmother could have grown for her 4H project. People my age remember fondly standing on our dad's lap and steering the car as tykes; today they take your kids to foster care and give you the death penalty if you don't strap them down tighter than nuclear waste in the back seat daily. And we wonder why they need to be medicated?

Victimless crimes are all side effects and no cure. It is our drug laws – not drugs – that beget gangs and violence. Minimum wage laws – not low wages – create unemployment. Closed shop laws – not right to work - lead to union violence. And all victimless crime laws inevitably lead to corruption of the officials who write, interpret, and enforce them. Homicide cops don't go bad; vice cops do.

Opponents of my campaign will try to paint our principled opposition to victimless crimes as support for teenage drinking, drug use, prostitution, pornography, pollution, vigilantism, anarchy, and heaven knows what else. I don't favor any of those things, and voters in Wisconsin are smarter than that.

What I do support is your right to choose how you will live your life, not have your choices dictated to you by others. Do you think that is unreasonable?

There are those who believe that red meat is worse for you than methamphetamine, and that killing animals is worse than killing babies. Don't imagine they are not hell-bent on forcing you to heel through legislation and judicial fiat. Think it will never happen? Who would have ever thought it would be against the law to smoke on private property, or wear your holster in your own fenced yard.

If the standard for criminalizing a bad choice is its potential for personal harm, family distress, financial ruin, and civic disruption, then adultery should be at the very top of the list. Its consequences have inflicted more trauma on more children than those ridiculously expensive car seats ever prevented.

Until the Democrats and Republicans criminalize adultery – and don't hold your breath – their zeal for other victimless crime legislation is exposed as transparently unprincipled and selfish. There is more money to be had trampling on the rights of a minority than to defend them, and it is as simple as that.

This campaign isn't about money; it's about principles and rights, and restoration of the ideal of Liberty that has been assaulted by a political class that lusts to rule, not represent.

Choose Liberty. Repeal victimless crime laws – all of them. Vote Libertarian. Vote for Tim, Not Tammy.

Lessons Learned and Re-learned

Note to business students: if you have just spent $50 billion to acquire GM and Chrysler, do not pay people $4,500 to buy a Honda.

The government's Cash-For-Clunkers program is out of money; it only took one week to burn through $1 billion, and now they need $4 billion more. That must be some kind of new record for government mismanagement.

This was the flagship program of Obamanomics - government/industry partnership, environmentally correct, economic stimulus, putting people back to work, hope, change, blah, blah, blah. It didn't last a week - and the bleeding has just begun.

Auto dealers have spent millions promoting a defunct program that has now been suspended. Clunkers taken in on trade must be recovered from scrap yards because new rules require disabling them on-site. State regulations will restrict this, so the lawyers can't be far behind. Every day, new conflicting rules come out, and more paperwork is required, adding cost after cost after cost onto the dealerships.

A classic case of good intentions meeting bad incentives. People who took advantage of the rebate were, for the most part, going to buy another car this year anyway. We just robbed $4,500 from Peter to pay 20% of Paul's new car. Worse yet, Peter hasn't been born yet, we just added the bill to his crushing debt burden.

The way the rules were written, the worst polluting cars did not qualify for the rebate. They are still out there spewing smoke and guzzling gas. For many classes of vehicles, the change in fuel efficiency gained from the $4,500 could be as little as 2 mpg. You can improve your fuel efficiency more than this by driving differently – you should ask for $5,000.

What is the lesson to be learned here? The same one we have to re-learn over and over again: the government is really bad a doing just about anything.

TOOTH FAIRY GOVERNMENT

Before we give government control of health care, we should remember Cash-For-Clunkers, as well as Katrina, Sub-prime loans, TARP, Superfund, and a thousand other debacles that did more harm than good and cost multiples more than we were told they would. If the government can't run a used car lot, we probably shouldn't let them try their luck at brain surgery.

In Article I, Section 8, the Constitution assigns 18 specific powers to the federal Government. These are necessary and appropriate – roads, copyrights, currency, defense, interstate commerce, naturalization, post office, courts and the like. The 10th amendment prohibits the government from exercising any other powers. Let's face it: those guys were smarter than us. We still don't get it.

In the enumerated powers listed in Section 8, there is no mention of buying cars, paying mortgages, running banks, buying auto companies, selling energy, running schools, or providing health care. Or about a thousand other things our government does badly on a daily basis.

Final note to business students: if you want to own a used car lot, do not hire Congress to run it for you. Get a used car salesman – they are more trustworthy.

Let It Snow

After nine days off due to weather, the federal government got right down to business Monday and took another day off for President's Day. How fitting.

The residents of D.C and vicinity endured nine days without government and one day without electrical power. Is there any question which was more dearly missed?

No one hopes for a power outage, but they are useful reminders of how important energy is to life and our standard of living. And government shutdowns remind us how unimportant government is. One thing is vital, the other irrelevant.

Which brings into clear focus the fundamental insanity of government energy rationing – it is the irrelevant depriving us of the vital.

Whether it is the courts imposing drilling bans, federal cap-and-trade tax, denials of permits for power plants and refineries, international energy disarmament treaties, or Wisconsin's economic suicide-note, AB649, government at every level seems hide bound determined to deny you your right to energy choice.

As a principled matter, you alone have the right to decide how much energy to use, what form you choose to purchase it, and for what purposes you will put it to use. You right to consume energy is embedded in the Constitution; the government's authority to stop you is not. Denial of your rights by force or fraud is unjust.

Government rationing and punitive taxation is the force part, and this whole Global Warming debacle is looking more and more like the fraud part every day.

And as a practical matter, government intervention into energy markets has caused more problems than it solved. I was reminded recently that whole greenhouse gas issue began when government mandated catalytic converters for cars; these devices convert CO, a non-greenhouse gas, to CO_2, the #1 culprit in Global Warming mythology.

It was also government regulation that enabled ENRON to run their scam; government allocations of various gasoline blends cause price spikes each summer; government subsidies for ethanol have messed up energy, food, and capital investment markets.

For nine days in February there was no Department of Energy and we all survived just fine.

Libertarian Party of Wisconsin 2010 Convention Speech

My name is Tim Nerenz, and I want to be your Congressman.

Not your mommy, not your daddy, not your doctor, banker, car salesman, landlord, insurance agent, teacher, pastor, union steward, or weather forecaster.

I don't care whether you are a Democrat, Republican, Libertarian, Independent, or only vote on American Idol, I want to represent you in Congress.

Represent, not rule. Whether you are senior citizen or a senior at the University of Wisconsin, you do not need my permission to live your life. Why should that change just because you elect me to Congress?

Most of us want a few basic things from government – keep us safe, protect our rights, and then leave us alone.

Leave us alone to go to work, raise our families, grow our businesses, build our communities, educate ourselves, practice our faith, pursue our interests, and take care of each other as we see fit.

We are tired of other people telling us what to do, what to say, and what to think. We don't need government's approval to be who we are.

We are weary of endless wars and interventions into the internal affairs of other sovereign nations. We believe in strong national Defense, not perpetual deployments abroad.

We have had it with moralist hypocrites – in both parties - using the power of the state to shove their beliefs down our throats.

Your Creator gave you a brain of your own and a heart of your own; mine can't possibly know better than yours what is best for you. Neither can Tammy's, Chad's, or Peter's.

I don't believe in the public good; I believe in the individual better. I believe that each person is a unique and exceptional being, not a helpless member of a herd.

TOOTH FAIRY GOVERNMENT

I believe that you alone are entitled to make your own choices in this world, and that you alone are responsible for the choices you make.

Liberty is the absence of government in choice. Government is the absence of liberty in choice. Tyranny is the absence of choice in government.

I choose Liberty. That is why I am a Libertarian. We are not the party of "yes, you must" or the "party of no"; we are the party of "hell, no!."

Less government and more choices: that's my answer, what is your question?

What is important to you – the economy, education, environment, health care, energy, employment, drugs, guns, taxes, trade, currency, markets, foreign relations, transportation, lifestyle, pensions, unions, social issues? Getting the government out of the way is the first step in fixing each of our nation's problems.

Limited Government - this was once the unifying principle of this nation. It is what we stood for in the world.

Limited Government was the reason our ancestors risked everything to come here. We have not just taken it for granted, we have taken it apart.

In my own lifetime, government spending at all levels has tripled from less than 20% of GDP to over 60% of GDP if you include the cost of mandates on the private sector.

Conversely, our economic freedom has been cut in half. We have gone from 80% free to 40% in just over 50 years.

And we are unwilling to pay for all the government we have. Taxes pay for only 58% of what government spends; we steal the rest from our children, our grandchildren and their children.

This is not simply bad economics, it is not a question of right or left; it is a question of right and wrong.

It is wrong to force Americans not even born yet to pay for benefits that we are unwilling to purchase with our own money.

It is wrong to force Americans not even born yet to bear the costs of wars we are unwilling to fund ourselves.

It is wrong to deny Americans not born yet the freedoms that were entrusted to us by our parents.

We are not the owners of Liberty; we are its tenants. The only freedoms that will be passed to our children and our grandchildren will be those that we are willing to fight for now. Each freedom we allow to be taken is gone forever.

Economic liberty and personal liberty are two sides of the same coin. It is foolish to think we could give away heads and somehow keep tails.

Both parties act like rights are favors granted by the state to groups who supported their campaigns. They believe that wealth belongs to society, not to the individuals who created it. They claim both heads and tails of the liberty coin belong to them.

Ayn Rand called it the great inversion: when the state can do as it pleases, while we must ask its permission.

The socialists in both parties who run our government believe that individuals exist to benefit the state.

Libertarians believe the opposite – we believe the state exists only to benefit its individual members.

We know that all rights are vested in individuals, an endowment from our Creator. We understand that wealth is like art, or music, or an athletic achievement - it is the rightful property of the individual who created it or acquired it in voluntary exchange.

We believe that the government must be constrained by the people, not the other way around. George Washington called our Constitution the "immunization of citizenship". We have disregarded it, and now wonder why we are sick.

TOOTH FAIRY GOVERNMENT

Government is not our master; it is our servant, our Cabana Boy. The Cabana Boy doesn't tell us what to do – he cleans up and he shuts up.

So shut up and go fix a bridge, Cabana Boy – and keep your hands off our money, our guns, and our stash.

Congress is supposed to represent us, not lord over us. We need to elect Representatives who understand that. Tammy Baldwin doesn't, but I do.

Next November, vote for Tim. Tim, Not Tammy.

Libertarian Party of Wisconsin 2009 Convention Speech

To paraphrase John Adams, Liberty is never killed, it commits suicide. For those of us who love Liberty, we can not simply lament its passing; we must act to save it.

When people ask me to define Liberty, I tell them it is the absence of Government in choice. People are not governed – choices are. In Liberty, your choices are governed by your own conscience and beliefs. In Government, those choices are governed by the beliefs of others.

Government and Liberty are therefore opposing principles – for one to expand, the other must necessarily contract. The easiest way to measure how much Liberty we have lost is to understand how big Government has become.

Government at all levels – federal, state, and local – will spend more than $6.5 trillion this year. That is $54,000 for each of the 120 million private sector jobs that ultimately bear the cost; the median income in those jobs is $38,000.

This year, Government will spend over 45% of GDP. Another 15% of GDP is consumed by unfunded mandates on the private sector. That is 60% of GDP taken by Government – by any definition we are already a socialist nation. Sweden spends 52%, France 44%, Canada 41%, Venezuela 30%. That's right – Hugo Chavez' Venezuela is only half as socialist as is Nancy Pelosi's America.

In my lifetime, Government spending has tripled, from 21% of GDP to 60% today. We have gone from 80% free to 40% free in less than my 55 years.

Reckless spending by both parties has created a public debt of over $11 trillion. There is another $6 trillion in unfunded social security liabilities, and an estimated $7 trillion obligation for the bailouts and so-called stimulus spending of recent months.

That is $24 trillion of debt obligations, which works out to $200,000 per job. We are stealing money from two generations of Americans not yet born. $24 trillion is half of the total wealth of all households in the United States – this is unconscionable.

TOOTH FAIRY GOVERNMENT

The current economic crisis is not simply a periodic pulse in the business cycle; our economy is collapsing under the unbearable weight of Government taxation, regulation, and manipulation of markets. We have created a corporate welfare state every bit as destructive for its wards as the social welfare state that preceded it.

It is not so difficult to understand how we have reached this point; for 2 decades we consumed more than we produced, spent more than we earned, and borrowed more than we saved. Government engaged in unwise military interventions abroad and unsound economic interventions at home.

It is silly to spend trillions in borrowed money to get the economy "back on track", when the track leads to ruin. No one in Washington seems to have grasped this rather obvious concept, but why should they? They do not value private prosperity.

If you recall, President Obama did not say "spreading *your* wealth around"; he said "spreading *the* wealth around". With that choice of one single word, he told us all we need to know about the direction this nation is headed.

He does not believe it's your money. He doesn't think you earned it. It was allocated to you, and allocating resources are what government does. The power to grant rights and dispense benefits is why elections matter, and they won.

He is not alone in his belief that wealth exists separately from the person who created it. Collectivists like Tammy Baldwin believe that resources belong to the whole of society, not to its individual members; so do rights and responsibilities. They are wrong.

Libertarians are the last vanguard of individualism and exceptionalism in America. We are not confused or timid about what we believe. Rights belong to individual persons. Wealth is created by individual persons, owned by individual persons, and exchanged between individual persons.

The purpose of government is to provide an environment in which rights are protected and individuals can reach their fullest potential, limited only by talent, character, and initiative. It is not the duty of government to protect us from our choices, it is its duty to protect our right to make them ourselves.

Libertarians celebrate real diversity, the inequality of outcomes that comes from equality of opportunity. We do not seek the common good; we seek the uncommon better. We do not want to be equally poor; we want to be unequally rich; rich in every sense – rights, choices, opportunities, wealth, knowledge, and freedom.

We do not want our possibilities constrained by some dullard's view of what is possible for him. Your success doesn't diminish mine – it enhances it. Your achievement does not take my possibilities away, it creates new ones. Your choices do not threaten me; they provide a reason for me to examine my own.

Socialists like Tammy Baldwin will never understand this; they are frightened by freedom, they are jealous of real achievement, they seek order, control, and sameness. They have no concept of where wealth comes from, how it is created, and how it is destroyed. You don't learn much by spending other people's money.

Let's be frank, Republicans can't win the 2nd District – there are too many Democrats in it. Libertarians at least have a shot. We are pro-choice on everything; we can connect with every single voter on at least one decisive issue of choice – healthcare, schools, guns, drugs, property, choice at 18, pensions, fairtax, military deployment.

My campaign will focus on the themes of Free Trade, Limited Government, Individual Liberty, Private Property – FLIP is the acronym that people remember. We will attack the socialist positions of Tammy Baldwin and we will propose alternative solutions to the nation's problems that are both principled and practical.

Our campaign will address specific issues, but it will not be about *how* to govern; it will be about *who* governs. I want you to govern your earnings, your family, your property, your schools, your life. Government should be your servant, not your master, and the servant has a job description – it's called the Constitution.

I know how to read it. Government does what we tell it in the blank ink; the white space belongs to us, not to Tammy Baldwin and her socialist buddies. I want to go Washington to take back our white space – I hope you will let me try.

TOOTH FAIRY GOVERNMENT

You can do that by voting for Tim, Not Tammy.

Marx, Robin Hood, and Obama

"From each according to his ability; to each according to his need." "Take from the rich; give to the poor." "When you spread the wealth around, it is good for everyone". It's not like President Obama thought this stuff up on his own.

At least Karl Marx recognized that people have different abilities, an objective reality that American socialists today can't seem to grasp. But at the end of his life, after observing his theories put into practice, Marx renounced them, writing "I am not a communist". He came to realize that exclusion of private property was a fatal flaw in his theories, because self-interest, not the need of others, is what motivates humans to produce.

And everyone has heard the story of Robin Hood, but most retellings omit the crucial detail that changes the entire point of the story; the money he took from the rich was stolen from the poor in the first place. The real moral of the story is that money rightfully belongs to those who earned it – we Libertarians have been trying to tell you that all along.

That leaves President Obama and Congress to be set straight about socialism. And let's just call it what it is. How else would you describe a tax system that takes according to ability and an entitlement scheme that distributes according to need? How is "taxing the rich" not taking from the rich? When you claim ownership of the entire planet to "save" it, is there any private property rights left to infringe upon?

How does need justify taking? This is the morality of the rapist, the looter, the con artist, the cannibal. Who taught us it was enlightened, compassionate, and progressive? Why did we listen to them? Why do we let them teach our children?

Socialism fails because it rests on a false premise; namely that people of greater ability will continue to produce for the benefit of people of lesser ability. They don't; they quit producing, and then they leave. Look around, many already have.

Each week, over 1,000 people leave our highest-tax states and relocate to lower tax states. These are rich people - the *most* able and *most* productive citizens of states like New York, California, New Jersey, and here in Wisconsin. Our "progressive" tax system will net 7.75% of zero once they leave, and hundreds of jobs go along with them. It's not like we weren't warned enough times that it would happen.

The capitalists in Texas, Tennessee, and New Hampshire are quite happy to welcome them, along with the wealth and employment these refugees bring. Who is surprised that those states are outperforming us economically? Did we learn nothing from the two Germanys, two Koreas, and two Chinas? Did we think it would be different here? Did we forget know how we came to be prosperous in the first place?

When Europe turned to socialism in the late 19th century, the United States was the beneficiary of a massive wave of immigration. Who came here? The most able, the most ambitious, the most independent, and the most honorable Europeans left *there* to come *here*. They came because we valued Liberty, industry, charity, private property, honesty, equal opportunity, faith, and profit. They rejected entitlement and sought opportunity. That's what people of great ability do.

Men of lesser ability remained to claim their entitlements and plunged Europe into economic collapse, war, pestilence, famine, and disease; hastening the evolution of their socialist governments into their most pure and brutish totalitarian forms – communist Russia, Nazi Germany, Fascist Italy, and Militarist Spain. It was not by accident that these regimes rose up *there;* the socialists were in charge. They have still not recovered.

And why now, do you suppose, that China and India are prospering? Do you think that two thousand rice farmers had a meeting one day and decided to build a toy factory instead of planting the paddies? Do you think a peasant woke up and simply guessed how to design an electric motor? How to construct a skyscraper? How to find deposits of ore buried deep underground? Did a billion Chinese people come over here to copy the secrets of American productivity? No, our most productive people went there. And can you blame them for leaving?

We drove them out. We taxed them and regulated them and told them they couldn't do this and couldn't do that. We stopped them from drilling, mining, logging, building factories, refineries, steel mills, power plants, ships, transmission lines, railroads, and dams. We told them they were less important than a salamander.

We seized the money they earned and chided them when they complained. We deprived them of energy, materials, and labor they needed to make the things that we needed even more. We called them exploiters, imperialists, polluters, greedy, immoral; we restricted their pay and forced them to pay us more. We called their profits "excessive", while our claims on their wealth knew no bounds.

We told them in a hundred ways they were not wanted here; and then we blamed them when they listened to us and left. We got what we wanted; they are not exploiting us any more.

Our socialist government is not just bad, it is deadly. When all the producers are chased out of this nation, we will be left with only the cannibals and parasites that lived off them, and a government that has no means to keep us alive.

That GS-9 over there at the U.S. Department of Agriculture can't feed you. You need greedy capitalist farmers, imperialist corporatist agri-businesses, and politically incorrect truckers to have food to eat. My need didn't put a single gallon of milk in the fridge; some unknown farmers' desire for profits did that.

And why should he keep getting up at 4 AM when we take 46% of his earnings? Will he go back to tilling his fields by hand when we cap his energy use and shut down his tractors? No, he will quit farming and we will starve.

Even then, Tammy and Nancy and President Obama will not admit they are wrong. It is not important that they do; it is important that they are removed from power before we reach that day.

This campaign is not about gaining control over the levers of government power; it is about dismantling that machinery before it is too late. It's about you reclaiming your Liberty from the socialists in both parties who have taken it away, bit by bit, over the past 50 years. It is about returning the greatest nation the world has ever known to greatness, so that the worlds most able come here again and we all prosper.

Vote Libertarian. Vote for Tim, Not Tammy.

TOOTH FAIRY GOVERNMENT

Math Reform

While they are at it, Congress should go ahead and deem us all millionaires – that would be wildly popular in November, and we could afford their Health Care Bill.

Where to begin.....you can't reduce the cost of something by 3,000 percent, even if you are the President of the United States. Once you hit 100%, the thing is free.

After promising a 3,000 percent reduction in our health care premiums in Ohio (apparently that sealed the deal for Rep. Kucinich), the President also promised us our employers will use that found money to give us a raise. I am an employer, and can assure you that there will be no raise. Just deem yourself to have received one – it's apparently the same thing now.

The President's handlers quickly tried to fix his goof, asserting that he meant to say $3,000 dollars, not 3,000 percent. Recognize that that is a 40-50% reduction in premium costs for the average employer plan, which is equally ridiculous.

Everyone understands that insurance premiums go up when the cost what is insured goes up, right? If you want $2 million liability coverage on your auto insurance it will cost you more than $1 million coverage does, agree?

Ok, then – let's do the math. The Health Care Reform Bill eliminates caps on lifetime payouts. Will your premiums go up or down when your $2 million lifetime cap turns to infinite?

The Bill mandates adding coverage for children with pre-existing conditions. Will your premiums go up or down?

The Bill mandates adding five more years of dependent children coverage to age 26. Will your premiums go up or down?

The Bill mandates insurers to provide free preventative care, increasing coverage costs. Will your premiums go up or down?

If you are one of the millions of Americans who choose not to buy insurance, you will be forced to – your premiums have no where to go but up.

Let's think about the other nonsensical claim that this Bill will save you money by reducing the deficit. The Bill is estimated by CBO to cost the government $940 billion, and it reduces the deficit by $130 billion. News reports described Democrats as "giddy" when they were told the cost to the taxpayers would be under $1 trillion.

I won't even comment on a morality of being "giddy" at the thought of spending nearly a trillion more dollars of someone else's money. But since the deficit is the difference between cost and tax revenue, reducing the deficit by $130 billion means new taxes must exceed the new costs. 940+130=1,070.

That is a cool $1.07 trillion in new additional taxes you will pay in addition to your increased premiums – over the giddy line, I'm sorry to report. There are about 105 million people working in the private sector these days, so that works out to $10,000 each. In reality, you can double it; nothing ever costs what they say it will.

Oh, but only the rich will pay, you might say. Think again. Who makes over $250,000 per year? Doctors do. Where do they get the money to pay their taxes? You and your insurance company pay it to them one procedure at a time.

When they charge more cover the added costs of their new taxes, do you think your premiums will go up or down? And so will the costs of everything else you buy, because for the most part, it is rich people that produce it and sell it to you.

Bend over; you might feel some discomfort……..

Here is more ugly math: an astonishing poll over the past weekend found that 46.3% of general practitioners said that if Congress passes the Bill, they would be forced or would elect to leave their practice. No wonder Tammy Baldwin's team is scared to record their vote for this sop to the big insurance companies, drug companies, unions, and trial lawyers.

And what business person will continue to provide insurance coverage at 15-20% of payroll cost when they can drop coverage and pay an 8% fee? None that I know. And don't count on a raise from your employers' "windfall" just yet, as it will not quite cover the cost of the tax increases levied on businesses this year.

TOOTH FAIRY GOVERNMENT

Still the President insists you will keep your employer-provided insurance and will not have to change doctors. Unfortunately, he is not your doctor or your employer, and can only fulfill that promise by putting a lot of guns to a lot of heads.

Advocates for socialized medicine claim this Bill will increase coverage, expand benefits, reduce costs, lower the deficit, expand choice, leave your current plan unchanged, and give you a raise.

That would be math reform, not health care reform.

Medical Choice

There are many reasons to oppose government-run health care, but we only really need the first one; the government will run it.

What is the problem with our health care system? It's not quality – we have the best people, equipment, and facilities in the world. It's not capacity – we have enough providers, equipment, laboratories, and treatment facilities to care for everyone. It's not distribution – there are clinics and physicians spread across every nook and cranny of the country.

The problem with our health care system is economic inefficiency – cost escalation in health care has outpaced other sectors of the economy. Health care and health insurance are two of the most regulated economic sectors; if government interference was the answer, we would not have the problem. Economic inefficiency in health care starts with the disempowerment of the consumer in medical choice. We consumers (patients) have very little effective say over what care we receive and what we will pay.

Effectively, a person only decides *when* to consume – i.e. when to seek medical attention for an illness or injury. From then on, we are pretty much at the mercy of what the providers prescribe, and what 3rd parties - insurers and the government – have decided we can receive and at what cost. Most of us do not even know what our treatments cost, only the amount of our insurance co-pays. We can not make rational economic decisions when we are separated from transactions.

The way to fix an economic efficiency problem is to increase choice and competition; add in the component of direct payment for services, and you have a Libertarian alternative to government health care – Medical Choice.

We already pay for many types of healthcare services directly – optometry, dentistry, chiropractic, many pharmacy products and services, routine office visits, for example. The simple act of paying the entire amount of a service, rather than a tiny co-pay portion, make consumers *and providers* focus on benefits and costs of healthcare services, just as they do any other purchase decision.

TOOTH FAIRY GOVERNMENT

Where choice and competition exits and consumers pay directly for the health care services they receive, costs do not escalate; in many cases, they have gone down. Who could have imagined $4 prescription drugs five years ago? Or $29 eyeglasses? Who could have predicted how inexpensive laser eye surgery has become? Free market capitalists, that's who. These examples do not come from the world of over-regulated, third-party-pay medicine; they were produced by consumer choice, provider competition, and direct payment. Medical Choice works.

The enabling mechanism for Medical Choice is already in place – untaxed personal Health Savings Account, or HSA. HSA's have been around for a couple of years now, but less than 3% of us can utilize them due to government restrictions and regulations. Uncapped personal HSA makes Medical Choice a practical market alternative to government health care.

Instead of others choosing and purchasing your health care plan for you, your employer or government plan would fund your personal HSA with untaxed dollars. You would then purchase your own private insurance and pay directly for health care expenses. You would also make personal contributions to your HSA, and your HSA could receive gifts from any legitimate source – family members, charities, estates, etc.

Insurance claims would not be paid to providers, but would be deposited into your HSA, from which you would pay your provider directly. There would be no cap on the size of your HSA, only a requirement that it be used to pay legitimate medical expenses for you or someone you designate – including charities that provide needed care for those unable to afford it on their own.

What does this accomplish? It eliminates 3rd party payments to providers. Studies show that up to 30% of health care costs are administrative costs, most of which are associated with billing 3rd parties for services, whether the government (Medicare, Medicaid) or private insurers. Many providers currently give deep discounts for patients who pay cash; under Medical Choice *everyone* would pay cash, and the overhead cost of dealing with 3rd party payment is eliminated.

In a service industry, the only ways to eliminate cost are to pay people less, or pay less people. Single-payer proposals target skilled physicians and nurses; Medical Choice targets billing clerks.

And as health care providers compete for your business, we could reasonably expect them to reduce their prices and fees and to increase the quality of service and care. When economic efficiency is the problem, free markets are the answer. There is no evidence to suggest that government-run plans reduce real costs in the system. Medicare pays only 80% of the cost of care; the balance is shifted to private payers. That does not reduce cost, it merely drives up the price of private insurance.

Medical Choice also decouples insurance from employment. If you are dissatisfied with the insurance your company provides for you today, what are your options? Quit your job or decline coverage. If you are on Medicare or Medicaid, you have even less recourse. With Medical Choice, you can change insurance companies. This completely chances their incentives – insurers must please consumers, not their employers or a government agency.

Your personal HSA would be an asset you own; it would be eligible to be passed to heirs of your estate, would be portable, and would not have time limits like Flexible Spending Accounts (FSA) do. You would decide what mix of insurance, savings, and direct expense works best for you and your family, just as you do with your automobile expenses. As you age and your circumstances change, you would adjust your HSA to serve your needs. You decide, not someone else.

While Medical Choice alone is an improvement over our current system, it would be even more effective if coupled with medical insurance reform. Government regulation of insurance inhibits innovation and flexibility and drives up the cost of medical insurance. De-regulating insurers - allowing insurers to respond to market demands for a wider array of products - is what will make insurance affordable and accessible.

That will be the subject of part II in this series.

Medical Choice – Part II

Socialists argue for government health care on the basis that Europeans pay less for health care and live longer. Yes, but they have to live those years in Europe, so that's a wash.

Europhiles and statists may be disappointed to learn that unhealthy people everywhere spend more on health care and live shorter lives; it has very little to do with who pays their doctors. Unless you propose that we kill them – which would provide the additional benefit of reducing CO_2 emissions, so maybe I shouldn't have suggested it – nationalizing health care will not make us healthy.

Americans are not particularly healthy people; and this is a choice we have made fully informed. In case you are an orphan who just awoke from a coma, here is what you missed: don't smoke, eat less, exercise, manage stress, floss, stretch, get your teeth cleaned, have your eyes checked, drink in moderation, don't shoot yourself or others, wear a helmet, wear a seatbelt, don't do drugs, practice safe sex, stay out of the sun. If you need more tips, ask your mom, spouse, or that skinny overbearing neighbor who makes *that face* if you light up within 100 yards of her.

In last week's post, entitled Medical Choice, I described a market-based proposal to reduce the cost of health care by up to 30% by increasing choice and competition and having consumers directly pay for health care services using an expanded Health Savings Account (HSA). In Part II, we will now shift to health insurance reform.

The solution for health insurance is hiding in plain sight. Let's think about driving. There are good drivers and bad drivers, and all points in between. For the most part, your driving costs are the consequences of your choices and behaviors. Your choices decide direct costs of driving, and you also choose from a wide array of insurance products, based upon your own needs, preferences, behaviors, and economic circumstances.

A family with two vehicles might spend $1,500 a month on driving with car payments, insurance, gas, maintenance, etc. $1,500 would not be untypical for that same family to spend on health care insurance, co-pays, and misc. out of pocket expenses. We have a need for both driving and healthcare; neither one is a right (apologies to socialists and teenagers). There are many parallels between driving and health care that are instructive.

Some driving/health care tasks we do ourselves – check the air in our tires and take blood sugar readings if we are diabetic. The amounts we pay out of pocket each month for gas and generic prescriptions is probably not so different. Every three months, we change oil and we get our teeth cleaned. Every so often we need a brake job or break a wrist – both will set us back several hundred dollars. Every few years, we buy a new car or have a major hospitalization - $30-60,000 let's say. And once or twice in a lifetime, we get sued for half a million, or have a catastrophic injury or medical condition that runs up into six figures.

Although driving costs and risks are similar to health care costs and risks, we approach auto insurance and health insurance completely different. One approach works, the other clearly does not.

The best template for health insurance reform is driving insurance. You choose to buy liability, comprehensive, collision, and theft insurance independently. Each represents different types of risk of unpredictable costs. In each category, you choose deductible amounts, coverage amounts, caps, and exclusions. You choose how much you are willing to pay, and you choose which company you will buy from – your choices run into the several thousands. The key phrase is "you choose" - not your employer, or the government. Insurers must earn your business, not lobby some board of bureaucrats.

Driving insurance crosses state lines; health insurance can't (regulation). Driving insurance offers plans tailored to individual circumstances; health insurance can't (regulation). Driving insurance varies with the number of drivers in a family; health insurance doesn't (regulation). All other insurances are regulated to insure solvency; health insurance is over-regulated to restrict benefits. It needs to be de-regulated to the same general level as other insurances are.

The driving insurance template can be easily applied to health care. There might be separate insurance for injuries (collision), catastrophic care (liability), and occasional illness (comprehensive). Your rate would depend on your own risk rating – just like your driving insurance does. Live safe, pay less; live large, pay large. A single person should pay less than Octomom. Just as most states have an uninsured motorists fund, provisions for a safety net must be incorporated.

There is another insurance model that can be applied to health care – life insurance. You can choose term life, whole life, or universal life policies. The premium cost is different for each type, and they pay out differently – lump sum, fixed annuity, and variable annuity. Let's apply this same principle to health care.

For a low premium, you can by "term" illness insurance; if you are diagnosed with disease x, you immediately receive a lump sum payment of y. You are free to seek any treatment and spend it (or not) as you deem best. Or "whole illness" illness insurance that pays a fixed amount per month for life upon diagnosis. Or "universal illness" that reimburses you for the variable costs of your treatments for life.

The novel idea of "term" illness insurance is transformative. It shifts every economic incentive in the whole health care system to outcomes, as every one of us will seek the most effective treatments at the best price. Innovation and quality would be rewarded; ineffective and inefficient practices would be punished and purged from the system through predictable market forces.

Like so many other things, improving our health care financing system is not as difficult as we were led to believe. In the previous post, we introduced the concept of Medical Choice – taking control for medical spending away from corporations and governments and giving it to consumers through the use of expanded Health Savings Accounts. In this post, we have added a conceptual framework for insurance reform.

In both, we have used existing vehicles – the HSA and the network of private insurance companies and local agencies – to fix what is broken in our health care system without sacrificing quality or availability. The central issue in health care is not cost, it's choice. Who will make your health care choices for you and your family? You, or a government agency?

Misplaced Outrage

When the world's dumbest owner buys the world's worst insurance company, nothing that happens afterwards should shock any of us.

Government bailout money is being used to pay AIG executive bonuses; yes, and welfare queens use food stamps to buy cigarettes, what else is new.

The U.S. government bought an 80% ownership stake in AIG last fall – over the 12 previous months, millions of sensible people all over the world sold their ownership shares of AIG. There is a good reason for this; AIG bet the ranch insuring sub-prime mortgages against foreclosure and lost.

Their executives say they didn't know the risk; since risk is all there is to the insurance business, that makes them the worst insurance company in the world. Or they are lying, which would also make them the worst insurance company in the world. No one in their right mind was buying stock in AIG in August of 2008.

Enter a buyer with no right mind – the U.S. Government – to step in and buy AIG for $170 billion. The firm responded to this ridiculously large cash "stimulus" by turning in the largest single quarterly loss in the history of insurance. And now they have paid out $450 million in performance bonuses; which the new owner of AIG, the U.S. government, did not know about until they say it on TV Sunday morning. For the past two days, every politician who could grab a microphone has been vilifying the AIG executives and managers.

Freshman year business students take a note: there is a lot more to running a business than shoveling a boatload of cash at the enterprise and scolding the employees.

The problem at AIG is not the bonuses; they are insignificant in terms of the total cash flow of the firm. From what I have read, most of the bonuses are contractually obligated. It is common for key employees in firms to be paid a lower base salary and variable bonuses based on defined performance objectives being achieved.

TOOTH FAIRY GOVERNMENT

Sophomore year business students take a note: when you buy a company, the time to learn about these contracts is in the due diligence *before* you buy it.

Employment contracts are inviolate, and a dangerous precedent is set when the government retroactively abrogates contracts. Sen. Charles Schumer proposes a law that will tax these bonuses at 100% - easy to say since bills of attainder and ex post facto laws are both prohibited in the Constitution. Sen. Grassley suggested the AIG executives commit suicide.

Junior year business students take a note: you cannot encourage your employees to kill themselves. You will get yourself sued into oblivion for saying things like this.

AIG illustrates the insanity of nationalizing corporations and other knee-jerk government intervention into markets. These guys have never run a business; they have no idea what they are doing, and with each week this is made more obvious. This is nothing to be ashamed of; it is simply impossible to manage the U.S. economy, and no one could possibly do it, not even President Obama and his team of economic geniuses.

Senior year business students take a note: when you own a business, you own both its profits *and* its losses. Our little insurance company is costing us $20 billion per month; and we paid $170 billion for it. On your first job interview, tell them you don't think this was a good business decision; you will make a good impression.

Markets are imperfect, but they correct their mistakes quickly and efficiently. Government does not correct its mistakes, it enlarges and perpetuates them. Its answer is always more of same: more spending, more borrowing, more taxing, more bailouts, more regulation, more hearings, more outrage, more nagging, more government, more scolding. And nothing will change; AIG is going to keep asking for more money, and Congress will give it to them.

As ridiculous as the AIG bonuses seem, I seem to be the only one outraged over what AIG does with the other hundreds of billions we are pouring down its rat hole. It pays out on insurance policies it sold to banks against defaults on all those stupid subprime loans they wrote. If the banks have insurance against their losses, why are we bailing out *both* the banks and their insurance company? And the deadbeats, too, for that matter. How did we get stuck holding three bags?

Congresswoman Tammy Baldwin voted for all of this ugly mess – bailouts, stimulus, TARP I, massive deficit spending, earmarks, government ownership of AIG, Fannie Mae, Freddie Mac, Wells Fargo, Bank of America, Citigroup, TARP II.

And Congress is where the outrage of the country should be directed. These guys messed up the economy, then messed it up worse trying to fix it, then threw up their hands and left it for Bush to figure out, then Obama. Now the Fed is stepping in to fill the vacuum, but only because Congress has done virtually nothing to stabilize the financial system, where all of this started over a year ago.

Throw 'em all out. Start over. We can't do any worse then this.

Missing The Point

This week's dust-up over who told what to Nancy Pelosi at one briefing she attended completely misses the most important point. The records released don't settle the lying score, but they reveal that she failed to show up at the 39 other briefings that the CIA gave to select members of Congress. That is the important story.

She was not just any member of Congress; she was the ranking member of the Intelligence Committee, the top Democrat on the committee with direct oversight responsibility over the administration in these matters. On her job description, this was the first line. Only a few members of Congress were briefed; we were at war.

When it mattered, she didn't even bother to show up - 39 out of 40 times. Why didn't Tammy Baldwin add this to her laundry list of things she wants her grand inquisition to look into? If we want to root out all manner of dereliction of duty, how can this not be near the top of the list? Could it be that Tammy only wants to hunt down Republican malfeasance? That would be petty.

While citizen-soldiers were fighting and dying halfway around the world, Nancy couldn't even muster the decency to go across town to do her job. Our sons and daughters are still fighting and dying, and both the Republicans and Democrats still lack the decency to just shut up and do their jobs. It is shameful.

The concept of limited government becomes more brilliant each time one of this current crop of legislators opens his or her mouth.

Congress Votes On Mob Rule

This week, legislation was introduced in Congress with the cynical title "The Employee Free Choice Act". It is not free, it is not choice, and there will be fewer employees if it passes.

The act is better known by its nickname, "Card Check." The proposed law would take away the rights of workers to decide union representation in secret ballot elections.

Instead, the government would impose a union on an employer when 51% of its employees sign union cards. This is a truly disgusting piece of legislation; it legitimizes mob rule as the de facto standard in labor relations.

Card Check exposes the first 51% of employees to threats and intimidation, and deprives the second 49% of any say whatsoever. This from a Democrat party that claims to represent workers and bloviates every four years about the sanctity of each and every vote.

The secret ballot protects workers from intimidation by *both* corporations and unions; it is fundamental to the right to organize and bargain collectively. Libertarians support the right of collective bargaining when it is freely entered into; we support fair and unbiased elections to decide collective representation. We do not support extortion, even if it is sanctioned by the government.

Card Check denies your fundamental right to own your own labor, exchanging it or withholding it as you see fit. Under Card Check, your labor is government property that can be allocated to unions and rationed to employers with terms established under duress. You have no say.

Card Check is so awful that socialist icon former Sen. George McGovern has spoken out against it. I'm happy to see there is an honest liberal willing to stand up for the rights of individual workers in this country – that's one in a row. Where's Tammy?

Anyone who has ever witnessed the tactics unions use to coerce employees into signing union cards should be appalled that Congress would give them a green light to fire at will, in some cases, literally. Only a fool would believe that companies will be not be targeted for political reasons.

I have been on the other side of union organizing campaigns in which employee property was vandalized, people assaulted, children threatened, homes shot at, women raped – while unionized Teamster policemen watched and did nothing. I've seen whole communities ruined when unions have shut down major local employers. There is a reason that 90% of workers choose not to join unions, and it is not because employers burn things on their lawns, it's because they know the harm that unions do. Congress does not care about minor details like will of the people.

One of the most egregious provisions of the Card Check bill requires the newly imposed union and company to reach a contract agreement in 90 days or submit to binding arbitration. Under arbitration, the government will dictate wages, benefits, work rules, working conditions and all sorts of other issues that get sorted out in companies every day, both unionized and union free. It is not so easy for professionals to do this, let alone some GS12 who just transferred over from FEMA.

Just think about how ridiculous that notion is for a minute. A government bureaucrat with absolutely no experience in running a business is going to dictate conditions of employment to a company he/she knows nothing about, in an industry that he/she knows nothing about, for an organization he/she has no personal stake in. Does any sane person think this might work?

It is not hyperbole to say this bill will destroy what's left of our economy. Credible estimates of job losses from Card Check in its first two years range from a low of 750,000 to a high of 1.2 million. I would argue the number will be far higher.

There are thousands of businesses that will choose to close down operations rather than permit their capital to be destroyed by government-imposed union contracts that quickly render the firm insolvent. Many more will transfer jobs to operations overseas to survive.

For public companies, laws concerning fiduciary responsibilities of officers to shareholders would require these actions in many cases. Courts would be jammed with lawsuits from shareholders, unions, employees, companies, creditors – all sorts of aggrieved parties.

Which exposes the real purpose for this bill; it is a bonanza for trial lawyers and big labor unions. Payback from Nancy and Tammy for the millions of dollars they have stuffed into Democrat pockets over the years.

This Card Check bill is un-democratic, un-American and it is anti-American. It is antithetic to the Libertarian principle of voluntary exchange, it is anti-business and it is anti-labor, so principled Republicans and principled Democrats should join us in opposition and outrage.

At a time when the economy is already damaged and fragile, it is unimaginable that Congress would even consider a law that would send jobs overseas, put more companies out of business, send the markets into another slide, and shrink our 401(k) s even further. And for what? To make union bosses and trial lawyers richer.

In a year of really bad ideas, Card Check is the worst so far.

Don't wait for 2010. Call and write Tammy now! Tell her you own your labor and she doesn't; tell her to stand up for you and to stand up to Nancy Pelosi. Tell her to vote no on Card Check.

Her phone number is (202) 225-2906. You can send her an email through her Congressional website http://tammybaldwin.house.gov/get_address.html

Money and Taxes

2009 was a pretty bad year for the Constitution, but 1913 was worse: it was the year that the Federal Reserve was created and taxing income was legalized.

I don't expect "Repeal the 16th Amendment" will replace "O sucks" as the student section chant of choice at next year's Badger games, but it is those students and everyone in their age group who would gain the most if we would return to sound economic principles of sound money and proportional taxation. All of us would be orders of magnitude wealthier today if those two mistakes of 1913 had not happened.

You won't find the Federal Reserve anywhere in the Constitution; it assigns Congress the sole responsibility for maintaining a sound and stable currency in Article I, section 8. In section 9, it even prohibits states from accepting fiat money (what the Fed issues) as repayment for debts. This was not a careless omission; the framers observed how the central banks of Europe oppressed the common folk and enriched the ruling elites.

The founding fathers knew that a central bank was incompatible with the ideal of limited and subservient government. For the first American century there was no central bank and we prospered as no other nation has before or since. Then, in 1913, the so-called progressives abandoned the Constitution and created the Federal Reserve, giving it complete autonomy over the money supply. Bad move.

In 1913, the first Federal Reserve Notes (the dollar) were coupons redeemable for one ounce of gold. Either one ounce of gold or one U.S. dollar could purchase a decent rifle, as was the case in 1813, a century earlier. Today, a decent rifle can still be purchased with ounce of gold, but it would take over 1,000 of those Federal Reserve notes to buy either one.

Gold and rifles cost the same, but the dollar has lost 99.9% of its value, thanks to the Federal Reserve and its inflationary issuance of fiat money – money not backed by tangible assets. We should abolish the Federal Reserve and return to the Constitutional mandate of sound money.

I personally prefer a currency tied to a BTU – unit of energy – while others prefer a return to the gold standard, and others a basket of commodities. It is not so important *how* our money is anchored, but that it is. We can not have a strong economy without a strong dollar, and we will never have a strong dollar while we have the Federal Reserve.

And while we are at it, we should also repeal the 16th amendment and abolish all taxes on income. Income is the product of a person's labor and no one else has a rightful claim to it. A slave is a person who has lost his right to 100% of the product of his labor; a tax-slave is a person who is 2/3 of the way there.

Before the 16th amendment changed it, the Constitution required the government to tax people, not the product of their work. And it required any form of tax to be proportional to the census, just like representation in Congress. The principle is simple: one person, one vote, one unit of tax. Equality.

That principle held government in check for a century, with government spending below 5% of GDP. And government only spent money on things that benefited everyone, since everyone was taxed equally. During the 1800's we became the most prosperous people in the history of the world, and not by accident.

In the first American century, Americans flourished because American government was constrained. In the second, it was American government that flourished while Americans were constrained. Our government now spends nearly 50% of GDP, and with unfunded mandates on the private sector added, the total is over 60%.

And our tax system no longer taxes citizens equally; it punishes some to benefit others. Our current tax code punishes work, savings, investment, thrift, and exports. It rewards spending, debt, taxation, and imports. It is not difficult to understand why we have too little of the former and too much of the latter.

Worse yet, our tax system insures corruption of the political process – it is the mechanism by which politicians reward contributors and punish opponents. It is how votes are bought

TOOTH FAIRY GOVERNMENT

in Congress. It distorts the markets and produces economic inefficiency. It screws the little guy. The current tax system is indefensible.

We can not immediately return to a proportional tax with the size of government that we have today; the cost of citizenship would be approximately $20,000 per person, $80,000 for a family of four. Now, you might be thinking this can't possibly right; you may not even make $80,000.

And that is precisely the point; the reason you *don't* make more than $80,000 is because the government has taxed it out of the economy where you could have earned it. Granted, some people would earn more of it than other people would, but that still beats Nancy Pelosi taking *all* of it.

This could never have happened under the original Constitutional requirement for proportional taxation, and it is why the 16th amendment needs to be repealed. It's why the 16th amendment matters to you, why the students at Camp Randall *should* be chanting for it to be repealed – but not at the expense of Jump Around, the greatest stadium tradition in the history of spectator sports.

But we can take an intermediate step that can put us on the path to ending confiscatory taxation, and give everyone a vested interest in reducing the size of government. We should scrap the whole system of federal taxes and replace them with one universal tax on retail consumption – the FairTax. In the process, we can dispense with the IRS, freeing up over $400 billion that is currently being spent each year on compliance with its ridiculously complex codes.

You can read all about FairTax at www.fairtax.org and you can learn about the movement to End The Fed at http://endthefedusa.ning.com/.

President Obama insists we need another economic stimulus because his first one didn't work. I agree with him 100%. End the Fed and abolish the IRS – that is my economic stimulus plan.

Money For Nothing

In 2009, Democrats raised the bar for fiscal incompetence - never before in the history of the world has so much money been spent with so little to show for it.

It is shameful enough that they stole our grandchildren's money to go on their fiscal binge; but it is downright embarrassing to see how ineptly they squandered over $2.6 trillion of future American prosperity. Money for nothing, indeed.

The list of blunders begins with the second installment of TARP, bringing to $850 billion the total appropriated for the expressed purpose of purchasing toxic assets from banks. How many of these toxic assets got purchased? Not a single one.

Next we spent over $40 billion for the expressed purpose of keeping GM and Chrysler from going bankrupt. And then both GM and Chrysler went bankrupt.

The $787 billion economic stimulus bill was passed with the expressed purpose of creating 3 million jobs and keep unemployment below 8%. Except that we lost 3 million more jobs, and unemployment is now over 10% and climbing.

Cash 4 Clunkers spent $4 billion for the expressed purpose of convincing people who were going to drive their old cars to buy fuel-efficient American cars instead. People who were going to buy a new car anyway bought Hondas.

And then there was the Mortgage Bailout bill - $75 billion for the expressed purpose of keeping 5 million homeowners from losing their homes. Oops – only 650,000 actually qualified, a small fraction of those were actually refinanced, and more than half of the loans refinanced went delinquent again within 3 months.

The Senate is about to pass an $871 billion health care bill whose original expressed purpose was to provide universal coverage, spending reforms, and a public option. After months of bribing votes out of individual senators, the final bill will do none of those things; instead it cuts care for seniors and raises our taxes by half a trillion dollars.

TOOTH FAIRY GOVERNMENT

Not to be outdone by Congress, the Federal Reserve *doubled* the money supply (yes, doubled it) in the last quarter of 2008 for the expressed purpose of forcing banks to expand credit in 2009. Credit issuance contracted by 15%.

On the international front, Copenhagen's climate talks broke down (thankfully) with no agreement on global warming. Somehow even that no-deal left us holding the bag to pay poor countries $30 billion for doing……..absolutely nothing. At least the expectations for this deal are realistic.

It would be one thing if Americans were clamoring for all of these spending initiatives. But opinion polls clearly showed each of these measures were overwhelmingly opposed, making them not merely expensive and ineffective, but also unwanted – the Trifecta of legislative absurdity. Tammy's Democrats passed them all anyway.

That is why the approval rating of Congress is at its lowest point in modern history. As it should be; those guys are really bad at this stuff. We all knew they were reluctant capitalists; but who knew they would also turn out to be such incompetent socialists?

Not that I would endorse government interference in markets, but let's put their foolishness into perspective. $2.6 trillion could have purchased 2,600 new Westinghouse AP1000 nuclear power plants; enough capacity to generate all the energy we could ever conceivably use for all purposes - *for several centuries.*

That's what $2.6 trillion could have bought – perpetual energy independence and zero carbon emissions forever. Instead, we got nothing, unless you count a one-year raise for some union teachers. That is truly pathetic.

We fired the big-government Republicans in 2006 because they didn't get it – they spent too much money, ran up debt, ignored the Constitution, and were drifting aimlessly in Iraq and Afghanistan. We didn't think anyone could possibly do worse in any of those four areas, let alone all four. We were wrong.

The Democrats have not just governed badly; they have trivialized the process of representative government. They have spat upon the Constitution they swore an oath to uphold; they have mortgaged our future to indulge the fantasies of their radical base; they have traded our precious sovereignty for the worthless approval of the failing socialist states in Europe. Thank God we have China to tell them to pound sand.

Liberals will look at this list of 2009's spectacular failures with pride; they consider passing any bill with a catchy title to be a great accomplishment. They are itching to spend even more of our money and shove even more of their government down our throat; we can no longer say we didn't see it coming.

In 2009 they have made their ambitions clear; in 2010 it will be our turn to make ours equally clear. Vote for Liberty. Vote Libertarian. Vote for Tim, Not Tammy.

TOOTH FAIRY GOVERNMENT

National Security

Our biggest national security threat is professional politicians who insist on turning serious incidents into occasions to play games and score cheap political points.

Case in point: last month's attempted bombing of an inbound airliner by a Nigerian operative with support from (apparently) Al Qaeda in Yemen.

Thankfully thwarted by an alert and courageous citizenry, it reminds us that the threat of Islamist terrorism is real; there are people trying to kill us, and they don't care if they kill Democrats, Republicans, Libertarians, or independents.

Democrats blamed Bush, Republicans blamed Obama, civil libertarians went hysterical over full body scans that haven't happened yet, and the TSA swiftly moved to strap down incontinent grandmothers for the last hour of every fight. Predictable.

The unfortunate fact is that none of these things will make us safe, and making us safe is the first responsibility of government. For Libertarians like me, securing the safety of our persons, property, and rights is the only legitimate purpose of government.

While we can't ignore the role that our interventionist foreign policy has played in fomenting disaffection around the world, it is delusional to think that U.S. provocations are solely responsible radical Islamist terror.

They don't hate us for what we do; they hate us for who we are, and they hate us for what they lack. Our courage purchased our Liberty, and our Liberty purchased our prosperity. They lack all three; there is nothing we could do or not do as a nation which would cause a single one of these cowards to suddenly find courage or discover morality. Their cause is death – that is all we need to know about them.

So what to do about international terrorism? What's my answer for everything? Less Government and more choices.

The mission is to identify, disrupt, and disable a loosely connected network of terrorist cells scattered across dozens of countries; to disable them *before* they carry out their plans. There are a few thousand of them, not millions.

That is not a job for the criminal justice system, and it is not a job for the military; it is an intelligence mission. It is the very reason that we need both covert and overt operational intelligence capability in our national security arsenal. An intelligence capability that is regulated by Congress, not run by the whim of the Executive.

It is also an appropriate use of the Constitutional authority for Congress to issue Letters of Marque and Reprisal (Article I, section 8). These authorize private citizens and firms to defend our nation from acts of violence perpetrated by non-government actors. Why should we not use all the tools at our disposal to combat terrorism?

Letters of Marque were used in the past to defend our nation from piracy and insurrection; recently Ron Paul has suggested we use them in the fight against terrorism, demonstrating once again that he is the sole voice of sanity in Congress.

Al Qaeda is to Islam what the Ku Klux Klan is to Christianity – haters co-opting religion to justify their own acts of terrorism. The Klan was not subdued by the virtual occupation of the South following the civil war; and decades of prosecuting Klansman through the courts had virtually no deterrent effect. The KKK menaced our populations for a century before they were neutralized.

The Klan was brought down through infiltration and intelligence work, using paid informants as well as government officials to disrupt and disable KKK cells before plans could be carried out. Blood was shed and lot of money was shelled out to private citizens willing to take down the Klan to earn a bounty; it was not pretty, but it was effective.

Intelligence operations and private bounties - that is the blueprint for combating international terrorism abroad. And we should not wait a century to go to work.

Private contractors pursuing bounties for known terrorists are more likely to dispose of bad guys and less likely to abuse the privacy rights of American citizens than are government agencies. The profit motive alone is a powerful deterrent to pointless snooping through the personal data on innocent citizens. Persons are only interesting to the bounty hunter when directly related to the bounty, while Governmental agencies have the luxury of dalliance that inevitably leads to abuse of power and lack of diligence.

Americans are a peace loving and civilized people. It is distasteful to even think about the nasty business of intelligence work and bounty hunting, especially when the mission requires taking of human life. We hope for a world where differences are resolved peacefully – that is the Libertarian ideal.

But peace is something to pray for; while security is something we purchase. And like any other purchase, choice and market competition produces better quality at lower costs. Combating international terrorism is a job that is too big and too important to trust to government; we must unleash our most potent weapon – free markets – and defend ourselves from the terrorists who seek to do us harm.

No Cap, Free Trade

The theory of man-made Global Warming has one basic flaw: the globe is not warming. In a nation with rational leaders, that would be the end of it. Not here.

In the early 1990's some guys with computers *predicted* temperatures would rise and all sorts of awful things would happen if we didn't cut our emissions of CO_2 dramatically and immediately. That is the extent of the science behind Global Warming - some computer models predicted it.

When the earth refused to cooperate and warm up, the Warmists rebranded their cause from Global Warming to Climate Change. That way, they are never wrong , and anything justifies unilateral economic disarmament – hot, cold, windy, dark, rain, fog, jet stream trajectory, too many bugs or too few, humidity or haze.

Can we please stick to facts and confine ourselves to Global Warming, the original doomsday scenario that started all this hubub. Not only didn't we cut our emissions of CO_2; we have *increased* them by almost 50% since 1995. And the temperature has not gone up; in fact, it has gone down faintly over the past 12 years.

Those computer models were wrong. The Theory of man-made Global Warming is wrong. But our leaders don't care. They are not interested in saving the planet; they are interested in increasing their control over your life. They want to tell you how much energy you can use and what you will pay for it.

That's what Cap and Trade is all about. It has nothing to do with changing the temperature of the earth. Even its proponents admit it will not change the temperature of the earth. The Global Warming scare is just a ruse; the "or else" that is supposed to make us agree to anything. I'll take the "or else".

And it has nothing to do with pollution. If that were the point, we should allow the construction of hundreds of new nuclear power plants – safe, clean, affordable, not one gram of airborne particulate and known reserves to power us for several hundred years.

TOOTH FAIRY GOVERNMENT

But then there was that one Jane Fonda movie, so now nuclear is forever out of the mix. That is how stupid this whole debate is: one movie and a couple computer predictions that have proven to be wrong and we are ready to take our standard of living backwards by half a century.

While the correlation between CO2 emissions and temperature is speculative, the correlation between energy use and prosperity is not. The United States does not use the most energy because we are the wealthiest nation; we are the wealthiest nation because we use the most energy. Energy = Prosperity.

We rationed energy in the 1970's and everyone got poorer. In the 1980's we quit rationing energy and everyone got richer. Those are historical facts, not predictions from a computer model.

Cap and Trade is exactly the wrong thing to do. China knows better; they have cut taxes, they are building coal and nuclear plants by the dozens, they are buying up all the energy they can find all over the world and they are drilling off our shores. Their economy is booming right through the recession, incomes are rising rapidly, and the best minds in the world are heading there to find opportunity.

We should follow their lead. We should *increase* our consumption of energy, increase domestic energy production, and remove the prohibitions on exploration, drilling, and alternative sourcing. We should lower taxes and remove regulations that interfere with energy markets.

We should produce more; we should consume more; and we should use all the energy we can get our hands on to do it. That is progress, and progress is the yardstick by which policy proposals should be judged.

No Means No

There are only two types of people who can convince themselves that "no" means "yes", and that "she wanted it" is a reasonable excuse: rapists and liberal Democrats.

The American people have quite clearly said they do not want government-run health care. Polls consistently show only a third or less of us support ObamaCare in any of its mutant forms. No means no to the public.

Running against government-run health care, Republicans have won a string of special elections in deep-blue Democrat states that Mr. Obama won handily – Virginia, New Jersey, and Massachusetts. No means no to the voters.

Even Democrats like Rep. Bart Stupak and 41 others in the House stood firm against ObamaCare over the inclusion of abortion funding into health care reform. Democratic Senator Joseph Lieberman and others steadfastly rejected public option. No means no to a few brave legislators.

Last week Anthem announced that California premiums will shoot up 39% this year, an increase mandated by regulation and approved by government. The latest ObamaCare proposal is so vague, the CBO refused to even estimate what it will cost taxpayers. No means no to the Congressional Budget Office.

But "no" means "yes" to the socialist Democrats calling the shots. Prepare to be violated. Knowing full well that what they propose is unconstitutional, unwanted, and fiscally suicidal, these maniacs are going to ram it down our throats anyway.

They will do so with as much anger, hatred, and loathing for their victims as any rapist could ever muster. Harry Reid's response to objections over his use of the reconciliation process – forced entry – was, "quit crying". Sorry our mascara stained your blindfold, Senator.

And they will justify their actions by telling us we wanted it, we needed it, it was good for us, we should enjoy it even. They will say we deserved it; we had it coming to us. They will claim we provoked them; prancing around half-uninsured and begging for it. It's our fault they couldn't constrain themselves – we are health sluts.

Too many Republicans want to negotiate with them, offering up groping and fondling in trade. This week they should have boycotted the crime scene; instead they will give the President and his media accomplices just the photo-op he needed to claim the act was consensual. Anything to avoid being called the "Party of No".

Libertarians don't want to be called the Party of No, either – we are the Party of *Hell No*.

We don't negotiate with political rapists; our message to the brutes is unequivocal: keep your filthy hands off me. And not just our health care; we want the federal government's filthy hands off our wallets, our guns, our stuff, our families, our schools, our jobs, our businesses, our churches, our clubs, our homes, our lifestyle choices, our energy, our data, and all the sovereign nations of the world.

We are tired of Democrats putting *our* money where *their* mouth is. We are equally tired of Republicans forcing *us* to show the courage of *their* convictions. Economic interventions at home and military interventions abroad have brought us to the brink of economic ruin, and the rise of the welfare state has eroded individual responsibility and deprived us of our dignity.

A century of government expansion has dimmed the memory of liberty and created an elite ruling class whose primary allegiance is to the power they stole, not to the people they stole it from. They are hoping we will forget what it means to live free and thank them for making us well-cared-for slaves to the state.

We have an answer for them: No. Hell No. Kicking and screaming and clawing at your eyes all the way to November, Buster - that's how it's going to go down.

Rookie

In a recent poll on President Obama's rookie season, more Americans said it was a failure than said it was a success. Only 39% still believe we should have elected him.

Even Massachusetts can't take any more of his socialism, electing an economic conservative to the Senate seat held as an entitlement by a liberal Kennedy for more than half a century.

This was a colossal rebuff of the Obama/Pelosi/Reid agenda, and the fourth pick-six interception the rookie Obama has thrown in the political red zone. First it was the Olympics, then the G8, then Copenhagen, and now Massachusetts. The media paints him out to be Manning or Brady, but he plays like Cutler.

Obama apologists dismiss his plunging poll numbers and humiliating proxy defeats, calling them the consequence of the President inheriting an economic crisis and two wars.

Wrong. They are the consequence of the President *perpetuating* an economic crisis and two wars.

Everyone that voted for President Obama (or didn't) in 2008 was fully aware of the economic crisis and the two wars. In fact, they were the only reason he won the election; his singular qualification for office was not being George W. Bush.

His 70% approval ratings a year ago reflected our collective expectation that he would do better. His current 42% approval rating reflects our collective conclusion that he has done worse.

His war policies mirror that of his predecessor, excepting that he has expanded the scope of conflict, increased troop commitments, and is even *less* able to formulate a coherent victory strategy, as hard as that is to imagine.

The right never did trust him on matters of war and peace, and now the left doesn't either; that is the singular bi-partisan achievement of Mr. Obama's rookie season.

But it is Obamanomics - not war policy - that is causing the President's numbers to drop faster than the thermometer at Al Gore's farm.

TOOTH FAIRY GOVERNMENT

Post-war recessions average 12-16 months duration, and we were already in month 15 when he took office. A President in a coma would have presided over recovery; *that* is what he inherited, Mr. Axelrod's protestations not withstanding. But here we are, still mired down in month 27, and this is all on him.

There is not one single element of the President's economic agenda – bank bailouts, purchase of GM and Chrysler, health care, stimulus bill, deficit spending, cap and trade, minimum wage, card check, tax increases – that is supported by a majority of Americans, or more importantly, a majority of economists.

And for good reason; they don't work. They didn't work in the past, they are not working now, and they won't work in the future.

We know this because we are *not* rookies; we remember the 1970's, and we studied the economic history of the 1930's before it was re-written by delusional Keynesians whose loopy theories were discredited by four decades of failure in practice.

The rookie Obama got schooled by the Chinese, the Iranians, the Russians, the Olympic committee, Pelosi, Chavez, Wall Street, Main Street, the Tea Party movement, and the voters of New Jersey, Virginia, and Massachusetts.

We all need the President to succeed, to learn the lessons from his rookie season; maybe he just needs better coaching, so here is my chalk talk for his second year:

Ok, listen up! We don't want government health care, energy rationing, forced unionization, and nationalized industries; and we don't want to be taxed to death while lorded over by an army of government nannies telling us what we can eat, drink, smoke, wear, drive, buy, sell, earn, keep, own, carry, burn, throw away, say, pray, and think.

Got that? Now, quit trying to force your throws into triple coverage and take what the defense gives you - that is the lesson to be learned from your rookie season, Brett....I mean, Barack.

One In A Row

President Obama's new policy on medical marijuana brings to mind the old saying: even a blind squirrel finds an acorn once in while. That was back when you could say "blind" and "acorn" was only a single nut, not an organized mob of them.

Let's give credit where credit is due – the President's decision to discontinue federal prosecutions of medical use of marijuana is practical, principled, and compassionate.

Libertarians should credit the President for recognizing the right of individuals to make their own choices in medical treatments and drug use. That's one in a row.

Republicans can stand behind the President for recognizing states' rights and following the Constitutional limitations on federal government powers. That's one in a row.

Democrats should be thrilled that the President has finally done something that is supported by a majority of citizens. That's one in a row.

You see? Limiting government is not only easy, it brings us together. The Libertarian Party has been way ahead of the curve; fighting for the rights of individuals to make our own choices over what we put into our bodies and for what purposes. Our stand was taken long before public opinion swung to our views.

But the President's new policy is a victory for a principle, not for a Party; credit goes to the millions of people who have worked tirelessly for years to bring sanity to this issue – people from across the political spectrum as well as people who could care less about politics and have acted only out of compassion.

The President's decision will bring peace of mind to millions of American families and it costs less than nothing – it reduces federal spending on prosecution and incarceration of people who pose no threat to civil order.

But one in a row is not enough. A Presidential directive can be reversed by the next President; or this one if the polls shift against him. It can be ignored by federal prosecutors. And it does nothing to confront the real imperative – comprehensive reform of our destructive drug laws. The President took one step, now it is time for Congress to get to work and finish the job.

The consequences of drug prohibition in this nation are far worse than the consequences of drug use. Studies continue to show that our drug laws do not reduce rates of use, abuse, or addiction. They have created new problems of crime, gangs, corruption violence, international terrorism, and the destruction of our inner cities. They have made a difficult problem impossible, and we have squandered hundreds of billions of dollars on a fool's errand that has now lasted decades.

Those who oppose this decision will worry that the President's ban on medical marijuana prosecutions will lead to increased recreational drug use. I ask them only to consider this: will you now start using drugs now as a result? Neither will I; and neither will anyone else who has chosen not to use drugs. And those who have chosen to abuse drugs are not deterred by laws – we all know that.

So congratulations, President Obama, I'm behind you 100% on this one. That's one in row.

Other People's Money

Now that the Democrat's forced march to socialism is full on, it would be useful to point out that socialism has never worked anywhere else before, and it won't here.

A century ago, the standard of living in Europe was much higher than in the United States; today, it is 25% lower. Why? Europe rejected free market capitalism and embraced socialism. Until recently, the United States has resisted the temptation to kill the capitalist goose that lays the golden eggs.

The fundamental problem with socialism is that its noble ideals of perfect equality and social justice conflict with the laws of economic science. I didn't just figure this out myself; it is the brilliant contribution to humanity of Ludwig Von Mises, the Austrian economist who exposed the economic fallacy of socialism in 1920.

In all of its forms, socialism is based on a philosophy of collectivism – the idea that resources belong to the whole of society, not to its individual members.

Mises theorized that the socialists' opposition to private ownership and capital exchange in free markets would inevitably destroy wealth, as these are the essential elements of wealth creation. He was right. There is no case in which socialism has improved relative standards of living.

Margaret Thatcher made the point more simply in 1979 when she said "The problem with socialism is that you very quickly run out of other people's money".

Mrs. Thatcher ended decades of economic decline in Great Britain by turning the nation away from socialism back to free market capitalism and private property. That gives us hope for a post-Obama return to prosperity.

The importance of private property to the prosperity of a society was recognized belatedly by none other than Karl Marx, the father of communism. In has last years, he wrote that the fatal flaw in his communist theory was the elimination of private property – communism could only redistribute wealth created by capitalists, not create any wealth of its own. And indeed, the soviet system collapsed as he predicted.

Marx figured out in the 1880's that taking other people's money is not a sound economic system; so did Mises in the 1920's, Hayek in the 1940's, Friedman in the 1970's, Thomas Sowell today. Not much argument among economists on this.

So why doesn't President Obama get it? Because socialism is good for one small segment of society – the politicians and bureaucrats who get to tell everyone else what to do and dispense benefits to those who curry favor. It's a good gig; and a lot easier than earning a living through competition. It's how most of Washington D.C. thinks, so it should not come as surprise to us that Mr. Obama does too.

If you recall, President Obama did not say "spreading *your* wealth around"; he said "spreading *the* wealth around". He told us all we needed to know about his mindset with the choice of that one single word. He doesn't believe it's your money. He doesn't think you earned it. It was allocated to you, and the rules of allocation are what government is all about. It's why elections matter, and they won.

He is not alone in his misguided belief that wealth exists separately from the person who created it – this is the prism through which all liberal Democrats view economic and fiscal matters. It is what distinguishes the collectivist from the individualist. And the mindset of the collectivists does not switch on and off when it comes to rights – those belong to the society as a whole, too. They are wrong in both spheres. Economic liberty and personal liberty belong to persons, not society.

Libertarians are the last vanguard of individualism in America. Rights belong to individual persons. Wealth is created by individual persons, owned by individual persons, and exchanged with individual persons. The job of government is to provide an environment in which individuals can reach their fullest potential, limited only by talent, character, and initiative.

Libertarians celebrate real diversity, the inequality of outcomes that comes from equality of opportunity. We do not seek the common good; we seek the uncommon better. We do not want to be equally poor; we want to be unequally rich. Rich in every sense – rights, choices, opportunities, wealth, knowledge, and freedom. We do not want our possibilities limited by someone else's dull view of what is possible. Your success doesn't threaten me – it encourages me and it thrills me.

The socialists will never understand this; they are frightened by freedom, they are jealous of unequal achievement, they seek order, control, and sameness. They have no concept of where wealth comes from, how it is created, and how it is destroyed. You don't learn a lot by spending other people's money.

It is not difficult to understand how socialism destroys wealth by separating the thing that is created from the person who created it, and then claiming it as a collective resource to be shared among all those who did not create it. The incentive to create is removed and there is less of the thing created.

How long would the artist continue to create art that he/she did not own? How long would the author write, the architect design, the musician play, the chef cook, the builder build? What inventor would continue to create new products with enthusiasm if the government claimed rights to each invention and decided how to allocate its royalties to others. The incentives and disincentives for wealth creation are no different than creation of other things of value.

Sadly, we are going to re-learn the lessons of economic history the hard way. Judging by the past year, our leaders are not quick studies, so it will take new people in Washington to restore prosperity in the country that showed the world how to achieve it.

That's what elections are for; I hope you will vote for me in the next one.

Poor People

Recently, a reader of one of my blog posts wrote to tell me that I hated poor people.

I was surprised to learn this from someone I have never met, but it did get me to thinking about why some people think that Liberty is a bad thing for poor people.

For the record, I don't hate poor people. What I hate is their poverty. And I hate government policies that keep people poor, along with politicians who prey on poor people and the play on the compassion of people who attend to their plight.

"Poor" isn't an adjective that describes a person; it is an adjective that describes a person's economic condition. Let me describe the economic condition of two people I am quite familiar with.

One is a single college dropout with a disability whose minimum wage income puts him in the bottom 10%, even working a second minimum wage job nights and weekends; he lives in a rat-infested apartment with roommates to make the rent, drives $50 junker cars, and can't afford phone or cable TV.

The other is a happily married guy whose income puts him in the top 5%; he has three graduate degrees, cars, boats, and motor sports toys that are paid for; he owns a big house in the country, a condo in the city, and vacations at his family lake home up North.

Do you think the rich guy hates the poor guy? No, in fact the rich guy *is* the poor guy, 30 years later – and both guys are me.

There are a few things that I know something about, and how to become poor and how to become un-poor are two of them. I won't bore you with my life story, because there is nothing unusual about it. Most poor people don't stay that way; and most "rich people" didn't start out that way, they earned their success over time. And what motivates people to become un-poor is that being poor sucks. The reader had it almost right – I hated being poor.

American ideal of upward mobility is borne out in statistics on the makeup of income quintiles over time. More than half of people in the bottom 20% move out of it over 5-10 years.

Just as I did, they work their way up the income ladder as they acquire job skills, experience, maturity, and more education. Those who portray "the poor" as a separate class of distinct individuals unable to move out of poverty are being dishonest, and I must say I find the portrayal of poor people as helpless victims to be offensive and a bit racist. A temporary lack of money does not mean lack of character or ambition.

It is easy to fall prey to hucksters who will tell you that the reason one person is poor is because someone else is rich. Democrats, especially, hold out the false hope that only government can end poverty. They are half right – government can close the gap, but only by making the rich less rich. Four decades and over $1 trillion spent did not eliminate poverty; if anything it had the opposite effect of creating a sub-culture of dependency upon the state that made poverty a permanent state for some people.

But anyone who opposes liberal and socialist policies is accused of hating the poor, just as tax opponents were called "racists", or those who oppose race-baiting were branded "cowards", and those who love liberty were labeled "extremists". We have heard it all: anti-gay, anti-children, anti-old people, anti-female, anti-environment. Name-calling simply identifies the point at which the challenge of an original thought becomes overwhelming for a weak mind. Some thresholds are very low.

Wealth is like music – you can't discuss it as a separate thing from the person who created it. There is an unlimited potential supply, and once created, music is distributed to everyone though the magic of markets. And there is certainly a gap between rich and poor when it comes to music – Elton John is musically rich, while I am musically poor. So why not rectify this injustice and spread the music around?

But how do I become musically richer if we take Elton John's piano away and give me one of the black keys? Give each of his 88 piano keys to a musically poor person and how has that made us a more musical society? Sir Elton becomes less musical, and thus the music gap is narrowed; but did that make the rest of us musical? And why should Elton John go create more music if we are just going to take it away from him again?

And why would some young pup hoping to be the next Elton John put in the countless hours of practice and study and risk of performing, making all the sacrifices necessary to become musically rich, if in the end, he will have to share those musical riches with me, who was unwilling to even practice between piano lessons for one year in first grade. There is a reason we are musically unequal

Wealth is no different – there is an unlimited potential supply of it, and it is created by individuals who rightfully own it, not by governments who merely confiscate it and redistribute it. We do not make poor people wealthy by taking the wealth away from those who earned it – we all become poorer as rich people quit producing wealth that they cannot keep. This limits the opportunities for poor people to get out of poverty – like I did, and like millions of people do every year.

We all become wealthier if we keep more of what we earn, and "spread it around" ourselves – spending, saving, giving to charities, and investing as we each see fit. This is what free market capitalism is all about; with all of its flaws, it is the best system yet devised by humans to provide prosperity, peace, and liberty for those lucky enough to have been born in nations who have embraced it.

Public Option Airways

Every time we fly we are treated to a dose of applied Libertarian philosophy – we are told to put on our own oxygen mask first before we choose to help others.

Simple principles, really: no person has a claim on the life, liberty, or property of another; voluntary exchange is the only just relationship between equals; you can not give a thing you do not have. This is sense that was once common; wisdom that was once conventional. Today it is heresy of the first rank.

Pay attention to this lesson in liberty while you still can, because it won't be long before the government buys one of our perpetually bankrupted airlines; after all, that's what they do in Europe. And things will be different on Public Option Airways.

For starters, on POA, there would be no oxygen masks, only an empty Oxygen Trust Fund full of useless IOU's. But don't worry – the CBO projects that there are theoretically enough oxygen masks to last until 2017, statistically speaking.

If there is a loss of a cabin pressure, POA would appoint a special commission, a Czar maybe, to regulate the distribution of masks that it doesn't own. Passengers of limited ability would band together and lobby the commission to receive preferences, set-asides, and mandated assistance - affirmative oxygenation.

The National Association of Oxygen Mask Producers would lobby the commission for requirements and specifications that would double the price of the masks and insure no new competitor could ever get a license to produce one.

The Eco-brutes would force the commission to mandate masks that are "green"; solar and wind-powered, with cap and trade filters that limit the amount of greenhouse gasses can be exhaled. Nancy and Harry would compromise on 8 allowed breaths per minute and write it into law, then add an earmark to build high-speed rail from San Francisco to Las Vegas. Ex-governor Doyle would sell them some Spanish train cars and make another killing.

Archer Daniels Midland would lobby the POA commission for the masks to be made of 15% corn; Northrup Grumman would finagle them to be armed with cruise missiles; the liberals in Congress would first balk at that, but then cave in once Dave Obey earmarked a new oxygen mask factory in every single Congressional district with some leftover stimulus money he had laying around. Rep. Murtha would get two.

The Bailout Banks would finance all that factory construction will free Fed money, and the projects would be insured by AIG. They would siphon off their bonuses in gold this time. All the pickup trucks at the job site would have to be GM, of course. A class action lawsuit would be necessary at some point – not for any particular reason, just to make sure the trial lawyers get their snouts in the trough.

Public Option Airways flight attendants' and pilots' unions would lobby the commission for a pay increase for the extra work of handing out masks that used to drop automatically. The commission would go one step further, requiring everyone on the plane to join the union, including all the passengers. ACORN would get a grant to sign them up with Card Check. Later they would be caught on tape advising Hare Krishna's on how to set up prostitution rings at all the major hubs.

When John Stossel reveals that there were no actual oxygen masks at Public Option Airlines, the POA commission would blame George Bush. That would satisfy the journalistic curiosity of the media.

MSNBC would counter with a special report on the gap between the excess number of oxygen masks on rich corporate jets and the critical shortage at POA. Jesse Jackson would cry racism, Barney Frank and Chuck Schumer would be back on *Meet The Press* speaking in tongues about the 47 million un-oxygenated, and President Obama would make a prime time speech, causing Chris Mathews' leg to tingle again, and Sting to discover God for the second time.

Another Obama speech? That would jolt those five senile Norwegians from their comas and they would give him another Nobel Peace Prize, the first back-to-back winner since Archie Griffin at Ohio State.......oh, wait, that was the Heisman Trophy, the one you must actually do something to win. Never mind that part.

And what about those passengers on the POA flight that lost cabin pressure? Oh, they have been dead for months now. But this was never about them; this was always about expanding power and control of the Parasite Class – the people who live off the ability of those who produce things and create wealth.

However, the flying public takes dying on POA more seriously, and they will switch to private sector airlines where a real oxygen mask drops in case of emergency and you simply put it on yourself. Radical Libertarians!

The POA commission will call them dangerous, domestic terrorists, racists, enemies of the state, and compile a list of their emails. It will mandate all carriers follow the same rules as POA to "keep the private carriers honest."

Would you fly Public Option Airways? Then why do you accept "Public Option" education, energy, agriculture, health care, transportation, finance, housing, and research? Where did you think I got the ideas for this amusing little fable?

We must quit pretending that government incompetence and impotence are rare side effects that must be tolerated to achieve some grand public ambition. Incompetence and impotence are the essential qualities of the beast; its only ambition is control, and there is nothing grand other than its appetite for power.

So the next time you fly and the flight attendant reaches for the oxygen mask, remember Public Option Airways and remind yourself to vote for Tim, Not Tammy.

TOOTH FAIRY GOVERNMENT

Public Transportation

The lesson from this week's Chrysler announcements is that when the Democrats were forced to choose between auto workers and UAW bosses, they chose the UAW bosses. Let that be fair warning.

Had the government just stayed out of it, Chrysler and GM would have gone through orderly (and lawful) bankruptcy proceedings sometime last fall, and would have emerged and be operating at a profit by now. Bankruptcy - A.K.A. the rule of law – would have given workers like those at the Kenosha Chrysler plant a chance to retain their jobs through negotiating a more competitive collective bargaining agreement, or even decertifying the UAW.

That risk of decertification was unacceptable to the UAW, so they instructed their legislative arm – the Democrats in Washington - to prevent it. One string attached to a $7 billion "loan" to Chrysler was acceptance of a restructuring plan that gave a 55% ownership interest to the UAW. Now, if you and I wanted to own 55% of Chrysler, we would have to pay something; the UAW received their stake gratis.

One little fly in the ointment – the government's plan required Chrysler's bond holders to accept pennies on the dollar payment on loans owed to them by the carmaker. They balked, insisting on due process to resolve their claims. They were demonized by the President for this position, despite their clear legal right (and fiduciary responsibility) to a lawful recourse. Nonetheless, they held out and the government took Chrysler into bankruptcy.

But the Democrats had already accomplished their objectives. By giving Chrysler $7 billion, they forestalled bankruptcy long enough to impose their 55% ownership deal for the UAW bosses. The administration said this week it would not seek to recover the $7 billion "loan". It also was revealed that closing the Kenosha engine plant and moving those jobs to Mexico was part of the plan since February. Nice.

Be clear about this, citizens of Wisconsin. The Democrat party that you elected into power purchased a 55% stake in Chrysler for UAW bosses with $7 billion of your tax dollars; it will be paying an Italian company (Fiat) to run it, and it is moving jobs from Kenosha to Mexico to improve the UAW's profits so there will be more money for the union to funnel back into the Democrat campaign coffers.

This is the same Democrat party who claims to own the franchise on justice and morality, to represent the workers and middle class, to look out for the little guy.

Only *after* they had secured protection for their UAW patrons did the Democrats push the company into bankruptcy, leaving it to the courts to deal with the collateral damage to suppliers, dealers, bondholders, and shareholders. Tammy's Democrats lied to us, lied to Republicans, and apparently lied to each other, if we take Governor Doyle and Senator Kohl at their word. Welcome to the club, boys.

Anyone with a casual acquaintance with principles of business and economics saw the Chrysler bankruptcy as inevitable last fall. They never had a chance, and everyone knew it. The $7 billion was merely used to stall the process long enough to impose the fix that saved the UAW bosses and their political machinery that Democrats depend on to win elections. That is the only thing transparent in this whole shameful debacle.

The fix is already in at General Motors, too. The UAW set to receive a 39% stake in the government's proposed restructuring plan. GM has until June 1 to come up with an alternative, but the Treasury department has thus far blocked any voluntary debt restructuring offers that result in a private equity position above 10%. Isn't that nice – the bondholders are trying to cooperate and the Treasury Department won't let them. Remember that when Obama trashes GM's bondholders in a couple weeks.

In effect, the government will accept nothing other than guaranteed UAW control of a post-reorganization General Motors. We have already seen this movie - just before the deadline, the government will impose its portion of the restructuring plan and then force GM into bankruptcy to clean up the paperwork.

Soon after, we will no doubt be reading about GM closing U.S. plants and expanding Mexican operations, and some low level Treasury guy will confirm that the government will not try to recover its $17 billion in bailout "loans" that propped up GM long enough for the Democrats to reward their benefactors. Some other governor in some other state will be screaming that he/she was lied to about plant closings. The administration will issue some feeble explanation, and Katie Couric will have to get another new hairdo so the media can change the subject.

To those who still cling to the fantasy that unions and Democrats care about workers and jobs, the Chrysler and GM deals should make you ill. They care about themselves and their power. You have been duped, and not for the first time; it is up to you to make it be the last. Tammy Baldwin has chosen between workers and union bosses – she is a proud co-sponsor of Card Check legislation that empowers the government to impose unions without an election.

For those who may have lost faith in markets, consider this: the once-largest and most powerful company in the world, along with the most powerful union in America has been brought down by a force more powerful – the decision of each individual person to either buy or not buy a GM product or GM stock.

This is the true majesty of the capitalist free market system; the least among us holds power over the temporarily mighty. You have more power than the Chairman of GM, the President of the UAW, and even the President of the United States. They could not save themselves from the exercise of your free will. All three of them together could not prevail against you, as hard as they tried.

This is why economic liberty matters; it renders might temporary. And this is why the Libertarian insists that government be restrained from interfering unnecessarily in commerce; Government renders might permanent, which inevitably leads to tyranny. The Chrysler and GM examples merely remind us of what we have known all along.

Vote Libertarian. Vote for Tim, Not Tammy.

Quit Talking Stupid

Are you willing to pay $24,762 every year so that everyone gets health care? Then quit talking stupid.

There are 105 million people who work in the private sector - that is where all the money comes from. We spend $2.6 trillion each year on health care, so do the math: that's $24,762 each if everybody pays their fair share.

If we include public sector workers, the share drops to just under $20,000. I know we pay their salaries, so it doesn't change anything, but it would be fun to see university professors and Congressmen put their own money where their mouth is for once.

It is nonsense to keep talking about coverage, access, and rights as if health care were free air. Rosa Parks sought access to a seat in the front of the bus; she did not demand that the guy in seat 12A pay for it, and she did not call him a racist for thinking they should each buy their own.

No, Ms. Parks did not talk stupid, like our leaders do. How can we possibly expand coverage to 47 million more people without adding a single doctor, and not have longer waits for appointments? That is talking stupid.

How can we possibly cover all those additional people without increasing taxes or increasing the deficit? That is talking stupid.

How can we say the 10-year "cost" of reform will stay under one trillion dollars by simply delaying enactment of the bill's provisions for the first four years and counting zeros in the total? That is talking stupid.

How can we say there won't be a board that decides what treatment you will receive under "public option" when it is already written into the legislation? That is talking stupid.

And when President Obama still insists again this week, "no one is talking about cutting Medicare" after the House Bill already cut it by $218 billion and the Senate is proposing $377 billion, he is really talking stupid.

TOOTH FAIRY GOVERNMENT

But we Americans are not stupid; we are pretty smart. We know there is no free lunch. We don't live on Planet Delusion, and we know stupid talk when we hear it.

That's why the most recent Rasmussen Poll shows 56% of Americans now oppose the Democrats' Health Care Reform plan – including a stunning 72% of independent voters. Only 24% of Americans believe it will make health care better, and only 22% of Americans believe Congress even knows what they will be voting on.

But none of that will matter. Congress will vote for something stupid that we don't want, they haven't read, and wouldn't understand if they did. They don't care about your health or your wealth; this is merely a way to reward campaign donors by churning out another earmark-laden porkfest. Quit calling it reform.

If Congress is not going to address the underlying causes that drive unnecessary cost – too much regulation, paperwork, and red tape - then all that matters is who pays, and that question is ridiculously simple: should we each buy our own health care, or should we each buy each others'?

Proponents of universal health care like this bumper sticker: "you should not go broke just because you get sick". That would be a great ad pitch for an insurance company, but it is a silly moral premise. Who should go broke, then? Or should doctors and nurses and lab techs and billing clerks all have to work as slaves for no pay, so that nobody does?

Here is an improved, quit-talking-stupid version: "you should not go broke just because *I* get sick". Treatment of a serious deadly illness can quickly run into the hundreds of thousands of dollars. If I am diagnosed tomorrow with one of these, and I don't have insurance to cover it, then one of us is going to go broke – that's how it works down here on Planet Earth, Tammy.

Why should that be you, and not me? That is what Congress is proposing, only they will probably beat me to the punch and make you broke before I get sick.

In Europe, they have universal health care. They also earn 29% less than we do, and they pay twice the payroll tax we do – 30% with no upper limit. And they pay higher income tax than we do, and they pay a VAT tax that we don't. So their disposable income is half of ours on average, and their unemployment rate is double. President Obama forgot to tell you about that stuff when he was bragging up how old they are in Denmark.

So how about it - are you willing to take a 50% pay cut so the government can run health care? Is it worth living half-broke your whole life just to squeeze out an extra year or two warehoused in a government home at the end of it? Not me.

So let's quit talking stupid about health care - and start talking seriously about real health care reform that will turn loose the power of market competition and give us all better health care choices at far lower costs.

Real Health Care Reform

As predicted, the two major parties appear to have fought to a draw over health care; now they will pass some watered down tweak labeled "reform" and both sides will declare victory.

Most of the haggling these days is between propagandists on both sides carping about the other side misrepresenting what is in the 1,500 page "government option".

I find it more illuminating to focus on what is *not* in the bill – any real reform. Three things in particular – tort reform, abolishment of government rationing, and ending prohibitions on alternative medicine – are conspicuous in their absence.

If cost is THE problem, then all the government has to do is indemnify providers from civil lawsuits in which there is no claim of criminal negligence. That would take Congress one afternoon, the bill could be one page long, and the cost for most hospitalizations would drop 30% the next day. It's that simple.

Indemnification would take two of the biggest snouts out of the trough – slip 'n' trip trial lawyers and malpractice insurance companies – and still provide relief through the courts should your surgeon show up drunk and cut off your foot. But you won't find impactful tort reform in either the Democrats' or the Republicans' plans – guess which snouts fund their respective campaigns?

And why do we still have the FDA in the internet age? It rations supply and keeps profits high for those already "in the club". It prevents beneficial drugs from reaching the market, it protects big pharmaceutical companies from lawsuits, it allows for all sorts of harmful chemicals to enter the food supply, and......well, just follow the special interest money and you can figure it all out for yourself. That one's pretty simple, too.

Underwriters Laboratories is not a government agency. Neither are the regional accreditation councils that we trust to accredit the schools, colleges, and universities whose graduates go to work for the FDA. Academic journals are peer-reviewed, not government approved. My Ph.D. was granted after defense to a committee of faculty, not a government board. There are dozens of examples of voluntary self-regulation of quality standards that are more effective than government boards. We don't need the FDA, we have the 'net – and it's free.

And where in those 1,500 pages of so-called reform do we find the expansion of choice through alternative treatments, holistic medicine, herbal and traditional therapies, medical marijuana, alternative credentialing regimens, and licensure? Why do the Democrats, who claim the franchise on compassion, and the Republicans, who say they are for markets and competition, both run and hide now that it actually matters?

I won't duck. My views on medical marijuana formed 30 years ago, when it provided my younger brother his only real relief from both the ravages of his terminal cancer and the side effects of the drugs and radiation used to combat it. I'm not ashamed to tell you that I bought his pot then, and I would again if I had it to do all over again. Why? Not because I approve of drug use; because I love my brothers more than I care about some politicians' burning desire to put Mexicans in jail in the 1920's. It doesn't get any simpler than that.

In two previous posts – Medical Choice, Parts I and II – I proposed a specific market-based plan to cut health care costs, improve quality, and expand choices. I highly recommend another excellent libertarian proposal entitled "A Four Step Health Care Solution", by Hans Herman Hoppe of the Ludwig Von Mises Institute http://mises.org/story/3643. There are many, many other good ideas out there; we should not be forced to consider only the false choice between a system run by the government or one run by your employer's insurance company.

There is a third alternative – a system run by you. You decide what treatments are best for you and your family. You make the trade-offs between cost, risk, prognosis, quality of care, and quality of life. You choose between providers who compete for your business based on quality of outcome, cost effectiveness, customer service, compassion, and earned reputation. Instead of lobbying Congress for favors, providers must focus on giving you what you want at prices you are willing to pay.

When the two major parties start talking about *real* reform - tort reform, ending government rationing, and allowing medical alternatives - then we might want to start listening. Until then, this debate isn't about health care - it is about more government, more politics, more crony favors, more red tape, and more of the same old partisan power struggle that will end in both sides getting a bit richer. Enough.

Real reform means less government and more choices – that is what will improve health care.

Represent, Not Rule

I want to be your Congressman. Not your mommy, not your daddy, not your banker, your car dealer, your pastor, or your weather forecaster.

That is how you are greeted now on my campaign website.

Represent, not rule; after all, it is the House of Representatives, not the House of Lords. Representatives are elected to represent a district, not an assortment of special interests that outbid another assortment of special interests in a campaign between two marketing teams competing with ad slogans.

There are roughly 700,000 people in Wisconsin's 2nd Congressional district. How can you claim to represent all of them when you are working to give some of them advantage over the others? That is the problem of big government, regardless of which Party is doling out favors.

The subsidy you give to milk producers increases the cost of milk for consumers. How do you pick sides between hard-working farmers and hard-working moms, when your duty is to represent them both? The answer is: you don't pick sides – you let the market sort out the price of milk, thereby representing the rights of both constituents equally.

That is why limited government is better government. Whether it is the economy, education, energy, guns, drugs, pensions, trade, crime, environment, or social and cultural issues, government expansion has turned us one against the other.

When government is limited, it is not necessary to represent one constituency against the interests of another; it is possible for a Congressman to represent an entire district fairly. In fact, it is the only way to represent the interests of all constituents in a district fairly. Including the 50% who don't vote for any of us.

There are plenty of things for the federal government to do that benefit all of its citizens; the I-90 bridge over the Rock River carries milk trucks to the dairy, dairy trucks to the store, and minivans home to reload the fridge. It is not a Republican bridge or Democrat bridge; it doesn't decide which cars cross and which get tossed into the river.

TOOTH FAIRY GOVERNMENT

But subsidies do precisely that. Tax preferences do that. The bailouts do that. Affirmative action does that. Health care will do that. Cap and trade will do that. Card check will do that. We have a mountain of regulations and laws that exist for that sole purpose – to decide who gets to cross and who gets tossed into the river.

You alone should decide whether or not you wish to cross the I-90 bridge, literally and figuratively. Not Tammy, not Chad, not me, or anyone else who might ask you for your vote next November. Our job is keep it in good repair.

So vote for me. I will fix the bridges and leave the rest up to you.

Republican Women of the North – Health Care Forum

Last week John Stossel chose the right word to describe the House Vote on health care – embarrassing.

It is embarrassing to know we have 220 members of Congress who are economic illiterates. Who are so arrogant as to think they can run the economy from Washington better than 330 million of us can on our own. They are fools.

I call it the tooth fairy coalition, politicians putting your quarter under their kids' pillows, and claiming they made us all 25 cents richer.

Believers in tooth fairy government will soon discover how a real law works – the law of supply and demand. Nancy can't amend it, and Dave Obey can't hang earmarks on it. When demand goes up and supply goes down, prices rise.

The House Bill adds 35 million people to the demand pool for health care services and it doesn't add one doctor, nurse, hospital bed, or pill. What happens to gas prices in Eagle River when all those Illinois people come here over Memorial Day?

Do you think there will be longer waits for appointments with 17 million more mammograms and not one new radiologist to read them? No waiting is why we have early detection, and early detection is why our survival rates for cancer are so much higher than those poor folks in Europe the socialists keep throwing in our face.

The House Bill is more remarkable for what it doesn't contain than what it does. No tort reform, no expansion of HSA, no interstate insurance, no liberalization of licensures, no allowance for alternative medicines. Not one of the dozens of practical market solutions proposed that would address the one and only problem we have with our health care system – outrageous regulatory and administrative costs. It leaves the current high costs fixed in place and adds 2,000 pages of new ones.

The law of supply and demand is why public option is supported by big drug companies, big insurance, big unions, the hospital association, AMA, AARP, even Wall Street. They all will reap profit windfalls.

TOOTH FAIRY GOVERNMENT

35 million new customers delivered for free to big corporations by the socialists who hate them – there is a delicious irony in that, but it is ruinous for the rest of us. So what does all this mean to you?

Point 1: your health care costs are going to go up, and they will go up a lot.

Not only because of supply and demand forces, but for a couple specific items I want to highlight.

First is the elimination of employers flex savings plans – using pre-tax dollars for deductibles, co-pays, and uncovered medical expenses. You will now have to pay with after-tax dollars, increasing your out of pocket costs by 20-50%, depending on your marginal tax rate.

The Bill cuts Medicare reimbursements by $400 billion. In reality, that will be cost shifted over to private insurance. And so will the un-reimbursed costs of those 35 million people who now be covered. When Massachusettes did universal care, costs shot up 33% in two years and many premiums doubled. That's the prototype.

Point 2: Your taxes are going up.

That $1.2 trillion "cost" of the House Bill assumes a 21% cut in doctors pay and no increase for 10 years. They must of forgot who wears the rubber glove when its bend-over time. That's not going to happen, so let's quit talking stupid.

And that CBO number is calculated with 10 years of new taxes and only 5 years of benefits paid – ENRON style. The real cost of this is going to be more like $3-4 trillion. That is the net of new taxes, fines, and forced premiums.

They say they will tax the rich to pay for all this. Who makes over $250,000 per year? Doctors, dentists, optometrists, chiropractors, hospital administrators, drug salesman, anethesiologists. Where do they get the money that pays their taxes? You give it to them, one procedure at a time. We just put a $1 billion tax on hospitals in Wisconsin – check your room rate if you wonder who's paying it.

The Bill has a special surcharge tax for millionaires – apparently Nancy can count votes, but not millionaires. Last year's federal deficit was $1.4 trillion. If we taxed every single millionaire at 100% we would still be $400 billion short. There aren't enough millionaires to pay for government *before* we add health care.

Point 3: Some employers will drop coverage and others will drop jobs.

It is simply amazing to me that the media has buried this. The penalty for not offering employer insurance is 8% of payroll; employers who provide health benefits spend twice that much and more. This is business 101, and we will drop coverage. Later the government will find you can't cover for 8%, and it will hike the tax.

We all watched cash for clunkers. We know the government will underfund public option, so we will all drop right away to try to get our people enrolled before the money runs out. It will be chaos. It took BadgerCare 3 months to handle 30,000 private to public transitions, how long will it take to process 40 million?

And for those businesses that don't provide health insurance coverage currently, the payroll tax increases their costs of doing business – in America. Foreign competitors are not subject to Nancy's laws. Jobs will be cut to pay for the new fines for non-coverage, and companies with overseas operations will be incented to move even more jobs there.

We have already taxed and regulated much of our industrial base out of existence – mining, textiles, shipbuilding, steel, appliances, electronics, machine tools, lumber, plastics, foundries. We can not survive as a nation that cuts each other's hair and watches ourselves on reality TV. We need to make things.

My company competes around the world against the best companies in the world every day. I don't lay awake worrying about what they are doing in China, they worry about we are doing in Rhinelander. What *do* I worry about? Health care, cap and trade, card check, combined reporting, tax increases, regulations, energy rationing, the DNR, the Department of Workforce Development and people like Tammy Baldwin, Steve Kagan, and Dave Obey thinking they know more about how to run our factories than the people who work there.

TOOTH FAIRY GOVERNMENT

The argument that they live longer in Europe on public health care is only half of the story. If the E-15 were a state, it would rank 49th poorest. Their unemployment is double ours in the best of times, and their average wage is 20% less. Their payroll tax is double ours – 30% versus 15%. That is 43% less take-home pay to use to purchase things that have a VAT tax added that we don't have – yet.

For the average American, that 43% is more than $1 million over your lifetime – that is your birthplace lottery jackpot. Maybe I'd pay a million for another crack at 24, but a repeat of 84 isn't worth that much to me. At that point, I just want to quit hurting and go to heaven, and I don't want some government panel in Washington booking my trip.

Rights and Entitlements

I am occasionally challenged on my commitment to individual rights because I oppose certain entitlements.

It is no wonder people get confused, when politicians throw the term "rights" around so loosely. I recently heard from a young woman who wrote to tell me should could not support me since my position against mandated employment benefits for domestic partners did not recognize their "right of entitlement".

It's too bad she won't vote for me, but she was correct that I do not consider *any* entitlement to be a right, and I do not believe that any federal mandates on employer benefits are ever appropriate. It's not about partnerships, it's about entitlements.

We need to separate civil rights from monetary entitlements.

Civil rights are absolute, unlimited, free, and universal – i.e. every person is in full possession of all of his/her rights at birth. One person's rights do not come at the expense of another person's.

On the other hand, monetary entitlements are relative, limited, confiscatory, and arbitrary – i.e. an entitlement exists at the whim of public sentiment. Unlike rights, which are free, entitlements come at the expense of someone else; a donor person must be deprived of the benefit for it to be conferred on the beneficiary.

The bedrock Libertarian economic principle is voluntary exchange – any voluntary exchange between competent adults is just, and any involuntary exchange is not. The right to own the fruits of our labor and exchange it or withhold it as we see fit is the right that distinguishes free people from slaves.

We also tend to lose sight of the fact that employers are citizens with rights, too. Whether a firm is owned by a sole proprietor or a million shareholders,

When the federal government mandates employment benefits, it prohibits individuals from setting the terms of exchange – labor for compensation - voluntarily.

Government mandates are one form of monetary entitlement, and they represent a coercive transfer of property from one person to another. That is the principled opposition to entitlements. There is also a Constitutional issue – employment laws are the providence of states, not the federal government.

The practical reason to oppose federal mandates is that employment mandates increase employment costs. Economics 101 tells us that if the price of something goes up, less of it will be consumed, and higher employment costs due to mandates reduce employment and personal income.

The expansion of government over the past half century has been driven by an ever-expanding notion of entitlement – spurious claims of "rights" to economic benefits that place a claim on the earnings and property of others.

We all have a right to pursue happiness, but we are not entitled to it - we have to earn it ourselves.

Rights For Seniors

I think it is wrong for seniors to be denied of their rights just because of their age; and neither should juniors, sophomores, or freshmen. That is why I support a uniform age of consent.

We would be appalled if Congress denied Medicaid funds to any state which did not prohibit 38-40 year old adults from buying red meat. Every adult has the right to buy whatever kind of food they choose.

So why, then, is it ok for Congress to deny transportation funds to sates which do not prohibit 18-20 year old adults from buying alcoholic beverages? Every adult has the right to buy whatever kind of beverage they choose.

The issue of a uniform age of consent is not about drinking. It is about individual rights and states rights. Libertarians believe that an individual has sole dominion over his/her person, and that includes what to drink. We also believe that states, not the federal government, have the right to determine the age of consent. In Wisconsin, that age is 18.

When I was 18, it was legal to drink. It was in 1980s that the federal government engaged in outright blackmail when it threatened to withhold DOT highway funds from any state that did not increase its legal drinking age to 21. Wisconsin, like the other states, chose to take the money.

Teenagers of my generation were no more responsible than our parents or our children. And most of us recognized the taste of our first legal beer, if you catch my drift. Drinking and being publicly drunk are two different things. The former is a right; the latter is a rightful subject for ordinances that protect public safety.

It will take an act of Congress to reverse the 21 year old drinking age strings attached to federal highway funds. It is not a partisan issue – it is merely correcting and injustice and ending the power of the federal government to use extortion against the states and deny rights solely on the basis of age.

The power to choose for ourselves without permission of the state is called liberty. We understand that; that's why they call us libertarians. You should be one, too.

Your Right to Health Care

Here's a good rule of thumb: if someone else has to do pay for it, you probably don't have a right to it.

Your true and natural rights – speech, religion, life, keep and bear arms, association, property – require other people to do nothing but respect your right to exercise them. Government can't add or take away from rights; it can only protect them or deny them.

But in recent decades it has become fashionable for government to fabricate new "rights" that can only be exercised by forcing someone *else* to do something. That something is generally to pay.

This year, health care is all the rage – we hear over and over again that we have a right to health care. No, we don't. We have a right to *purchase* health care.

Health care is not an element on the periodic table; it is something that one person produces and another consumes. No person can claim a right to the fruits of another person's labor; that is called slavery.

And advocates of socialized medicine don't stop at inventing a right to health care; they insist you have a right to *affordable* health care. Affordable health care is the kind that someone else pays for. Making someone else pay does not make something affordable; it just makes it affordable for you. So does stealing it.

But Tim, you might argue, health care is different than other products – you need it to live. Ok, next February you call and make an appointment to see your doctor; then go stand outside naked without eating or drinking until it's time for your exam. You will freeze, starve, or die of thirst long before they start wondering why you didn't show up for your colonoscopy.

You need lots of things to live. You have a right to purchase food; you don't have the right to take it from someone else. You have a right to purchase water, not steal it from your neighbor. You have a right to purchase housing, not to camp out in my living room. You have the right to purchase clothes, not shoplift

TOOTH FAIRY GOVERNMENT

from the Gap. You have the right to purchase energy, not to siphon gas from parked cars.

If the government has to provide anything you have a right to but can't/won't buy for yourself, then why not start with the second amendment. There are probably more Americans unarmed than uninsured, so shouldn't we take care of explicit Constitutional rights before we move on the ones we can't even define?

What health care exactly do we have a right to? Each of us would draw a line a bit differently along a spectrum of procedures that ranges from check-up to gender reassignment. Think we can reach a consensus on what health care is? We can't even reach a consensus on when life starts, let alone what it rights attend to it.

The Problem with Government

The problem with government is that there is too much of it; we resent how much we must pay for it, and we resent even more how much attention we must pay to it.

Most of us would rather spend our money, time, and energy on work, family, friends, church, hobbies, entertainment, education, homes, sports, communities, and about 100 other things that are higher up on our priority list. But government has become too big to avoid – it is inescapable.

Not only is government intervening into every little nook and cranny of our lives, but that involvement is intensely politicized – the mandates, permissions, subsidies, and penalties that government attaches to daily living are driven by ideology, and justified (or opposed) by spin, half-truths, wild exaggerations, and outright lies.

It is exhausting just to weed through all that crap to form an independent opinion on any particular issue. Facts are hard to come by once our elected officials and media pundits start posturing, posing, and screaming hysterically about bills they have not read, proposals that haven't been written, and ideas they can't comprehend.

Government was not meant to be exhausting. It was meant to be… there. Like elevator music, or white noise, or the other four guys in the Dave Clark Five. We-the-people are supposed to be Oprah and the government is supposed to be Steadman, not the other way around.

The founding fathers decided on a federal government of limited, enumerated, and carefully balanced powers. Their challenges were far worse than ours – health care, elderly care, poverty, unemployment, border security, education, energy, ethnic tensions, religious expression – but they understood that government causes more problems than it cures. History has proven them to be right.

The whole idea of limited government is for us to live our lives free from the politicians' constant demands to be the center of our attention every single day. When we speak of freedom and independence, we mean freedom *from* government and

TOOTH FAIRY GOVERNMENT

independence *from* government. Liberty is the *absence* of government in choice. The less relevant government is, the more relevant you become.

And when we do pay attention to government – kicking and screaming - we don't like what we see; like SEC regulators watching porn on our dime, for example. Or that the average federal government employee makes $119,000 per year – double the average of the private sector. Or that the total number of all government employees (22 million) now exceeds the number of people who make things in this country – manufacturing, agriculture, mining, and construction combined.

There's your problem with government: too much jockey, not enough horse.

It doesn't matter whether the jockey is holding the whip in his Left hand or his Right; the problem is that he weighs over 600 pounds – that is the ratio of government spending in our $1.4 trillion thoroughbred economy. We wonder why we are losing the race for global competitiveness.

Each new tax is one less bag of oats for the starving racehorse and another batch of oatmeal cookies down the gaping pie hole of the bloated government jockey. Each new regulation is another bucket of water taken from the thirsty steed to satisfy the hulking mass of sweaty satin that is breaking the back of our nation.

The solution for the problem of too much government is not complicated: feed the horse and starve the jockey. Repeal regulations, reduce spending, reduce taxes, reduce borrowing, and de-criminalize free will. It is not enough to simply change from one fat jockey to the fat jockey of the other party every few years; we must cut the government down to size before we can claim once again to be a free people.

You were not put on this earth to pull another man's plow; you were born to run. To run free and proud, as fast and as far as your talent, ambition, character, choices, associations, and good fortune will take you. Liberty is the wind in your face; government promises the collective dull plodding of the 40 horse team.

Only the wild stallions run free; the plow horse must be broken before it will submit to the yoke. Do not submit. Throw off the yoke. Reclaim your Liberty.

TOOTH FAIRY GOVERNMENT

Pool Boy

Your family makes $140,000. You pay your pool boy $24,000 and he spends $38,000. He is $130,000 in debt and he tells lenders *you* are good for it. Now do you get the Tea Party?

If you remember who works for whom and where the money comes from in the first place, it is pretty easy to see why people are hacked off. Add eight zeros to the pool boy's numbers and you have the budget of the federal government.

The government works for us; the pool boy is not family. We pay him $2.4 trillion in taxes to keep up the house and grounds so we can go to work. His job description is the Constitution; it tells him what he can and can't to do out in the yard and it warns him to stay out of the house in about 10 different places.

We Americans produce about $14 trillion of goods and services each year - that is our national GDP. Wealth is like food, somebody has to make the stuff so the rest of us can eat. That is what the private sector does – we make all the money that everybody spends. It's our money; it does not belong to the pool boy.

The pool boy tries to hide his desperate financial straits by stating *his* deficits and debt as a percentage of *our* GDP. When he says he is running a deficit of 9% of our GDP it doesn't sound as asinine as overspending his own revenues by 78%. The pool boy's debt is 541% of his own income; he would prefer to say 90% of our GDP. That sounds asinine no matter how you say it.

Most of us would cut back on our spending; not the pool boy. He formed his own union many years ago, so now he negotiates with himself. No surprise he has secured better wages, benefits, pensions, and tenure. The average federal government worker now makes $119,000 - more than *twice* the private sector average – and they get to watch porn all day without getting fired.

Why are people angry? Our pool boy costs too much, he steals our kid's money, he lies to us, and he doesn't do squat. That's why.

This is not about race, religion, party affiliation, or repealing 50 year-old laws. It is about the looting of America by public unions, special interests, corporate welfare queens, warmongers, socialists, tax cheats, banksters, and every other species of ungrateful civic parasite who thinks self-government means they get to write checks to themselves.

I frankly don't understand people who are *not* angry. And I feel sorry for well-meaning liberals who put their faith in the pool boy; they are forced to choose each day between denial and heartbreak as a government too big NOT to fail puts its reliable incompetence on full display. Even James Carville has had enough.

Want to know why people are terrified watching the oil spew out of the ocean floor for the 42nd day in a row? Because we know that someday that will be a blown heart valve or an ulcerated colon, and it won't be pelicans dying while the government dithers.

Want to know why people are having second thoughts about giving our entire health care system over to an advisory commission appointed by the President? Because we just learned that the only qualification for this sort of job is to not run against some fossilized incumbent hack in a primary.

Libertarians have never trusted the pool boy. We don't care if he's holding the skimming net in his left hand or his right; the only difference between a leftie and a rightie is what he would take away first after he breaks into the house. People used to think we were nuts to worry; not so much anymore.

Anger need not turn to panic. We elect a new bunch of pool boys every two years, and we can send folks to Washington who will scoop out the turds, skim off the scum, change the filters, and restart the circulating pumps.

It won't take long and the pool will be clean and clear, but only if we stay angry all the way to November.

Arrested Development

The Civil Rights Act of 1964? Why do we have to reopen that debate because of something one guy didn't say on a program no one watched?

And wasn't the name of their website MoveOn? Whatever happened to that idea?

We are now in the *fourth* year of Democratic control in Congress, and they are still whining about GWB instead of doing the job we pay them for.

It has been *thirty* years since Ronald Reagan's tax cuts were proposed, and I am still reading about how the current deficit and debt crises we face are his fault.

It has been *forty-six* years since the Civil Rights Act was passed and now we have to spend all summer listening to a bunch of liberal racists-in-remission scold the rest of us who never had their disease.

The economy still sucks, the market is taking a dump, unemployment is going up, Europe is imploding, we are stuck in two wars without identifiable victory strategies, and we are going to take the summer off to play dress-up with civil-rights-Barbie.

I have a theory for why the left is obsessed with the conflicts of their childhood – particularly race. I blame Dr. Spock.

Before he convinced our parents not to spank, parents *corrected* their children. You made a mistake, you got a love tap, and you – listen up, lefties – MOVED ON. You quit doing naughty things and went back outside to play with your friends.

After Spock, you got to sit by yourself and contemplate your guilt and shame during your time out, confused about what you did wrong, and building up rage against the happy kids that were back playing outside. There was no closure, so you obsessed about those naughty things, convincing yourself that everyone is bad and needs to be fixed.

So that's my theory of where liberal whackjobs come from – they obsess about the past and insist that we join them in the corner for a perpetual national timeout.

And far-right wingnuts were probably beaten as kids – they act out their mother-loathing by invading defenseless countries, wire-tapping, throwing people in jail, and selling derivatives.

The majority of Americans are the happy kids that just want to play outside – Libertarians certainly are down with that. We are the party of playing outside.

We happy kids are adults now; when we mess up, we take our spanking, quit doing naughty things, and we – listen up again, lefties - MOVE ON. We are sick and tired of taking orders from you beaten kids and you fixated neurotic kids who can't get the hang of it.

Go fix yourself. Get a grip. Get some help. Pull your head out. Go to church if you want forgiveness. Start a 12-step, and then add step #13: leave us alone.

It's just a theory.

Independence Revisited

It is a uniquely American holiday, this Independence Day; it is the day we commemorate the abolishment of our government.

This nation did not materialize from the vapor one day in 1776. There was nearly 200 years of colonial life, and there was government for all of that time. We did not create a new government on that Fourth of July; we just dissolved the old one.

The national holiday which commemorates our disposal of unwanted government is properly called Independence Day. It does not commemorate independence from our parents, from want, from ignorance, from an addiction, or from a relationship gone sour; it is a celebration of our independence *from government*.

How appropriate that our Independence Day celebrations include illegal fireworks, noise violations, public overindulgence, teeth-rattling Harleys with helmetless riders, music blasting at annoying decibels, wake-roiling boat parades, broken curfews, and all manner of hoopla that is likely illegal and certainly bad for you.

That's what liberty looks like - every conceivable form of happiness being publically pursued under one proudly waved flag. Is it so unbearable? We Libertarians would let 'er rip the other 364 days of the year if we had our druthers. Pray, play, or work all day – whatever floats your boat.

The government that was tossed aside in 1776 did not originate the idea of self-rule; it did not confer sovereignty upon its citizens, and it did not find the truth of natural rights to be self-evident, an endowment from the Creator. That government claimed the Creator himself gave it the power to rule; it deemed itself the arbiter of goodness and the provider of the general welfare. It rejected the notion of "consent of the governed", and it considered the wealth of the people to be its own.

That government was not reformed, it was not streamlined, it was not constrained, it was not tilted to the right or left of its center - it was *abolished*. And it would be 13 years before the Constitution would empower another in 1789.

Who can imagine dissolving our government this July 4th and not constituting a replacement until 2023? This truly was the home of the brave....once.

They abolished the entire government, while we are afraid to abolish the Department of Education. They fought and died for their freedom, while we won't bother to vote for ours. They sacked the entire bureaucracy, while we are afraid to limit their raises. They gave government 13 years off and we freak out over a furlough day.

What happened to us? When did we give up on ourselves? Why do we believe that we are incapable of individual sovereignty, unfit for self-rule? Who is teaching us that we are less worthy of liberty than our foreparents? Why do we listen to these people? Why do we elect them to speak for us?

The colonials were no different from us; we are separated only by time, technology and fashion. Their civic challenges – trade, security, employment, energy, education, health, charity, foreign relations, poverty, homelessness, crime, pollution, nutrition, elder care – were far more daunting than anything we face today, while their means of coping were primitive by our standards.

And after thirteen freezing winters, thirteen blazing summers, thirteen deadly influenza seasons, and thirteen years of unregulated business cycles, did they run back to government for protection? Did you run back to Mommy and Daddy's once you moved out? Neither did they.

They created a federal government that was strictly limited, that preserved liberty to the maximum extent practical in an ordered society of peaceful citizens. Not on a whim, not on a theory, but after thirteen years of living free and facing the consequences with eyes wide open. They found the benefits of liberty so far outweighed the costs they forbid government from encroaching on it legally.

Our task is far less demanding, and we do not need to take up arms to abolish our government; our founders provided the opportunity for a revolution every two years via the ballot box - another mulligan every even-numbered year.

We have strayed far from the path of liberty. We moved back in with Mommy and Daddy and now we resent living in the basement under their rules. It is not their fault that we seethe, it is ours; we need to move out and make it on our own. And we will all get along much better with Mommy and Daddy when we just stop by to visit from time to time.

It is our turn to declare our independence from government, just as our predecessors did in 1776. The clear lesson of history is that freedom and prosperity are inexorably linked, while tyranny and poverty are equally certain companions. We are known by the company we keep.

On July 4, 1776, our founders chose the former and rejected the latter. We don't even have to find the words, we just need to repeat them: *"We find these truths to be self evident....."*

Each of us will be remembered for what we did, not for what we hoped to do; this November we will be remembered for either restoring our liberty and to securing the prosperity of generations to come, or for failing to do so when we knew it was our last chance.

As we celebrate this Independence Day with our family and friends, let us commit ourselves to reclaiming our liberty. With each illegal firework, let us remember what it is we are celebrating – our independence *from* government.

Happy Independence Day!

Counting Snouts

In my speech at the AFP Town Hall Meetings in August, I used the phrase "snouts in the trough" to describe trial lawyers and malpractice insurers. An apology is owed; no, not to them, but to all the other snouts who were not given their due.

When I go to see my doctor, he spends a few minutes with me reviewing my vitals, asking how I feel, and renewing my prescriptions. If I paid him $15 cash, he could earn over $300,000 at that rate; and I would cut my cost of health care by 80%. We would both be happy.

Michael Moore, if you are reading this, that is how capitalism works: a voluntary exchange makes both parties happy and everyone else minds their own business. But that's not how health care works. Oh, no. There are a few more snouts in the trough and it is everybody else's business. Let's count snouts.

Just in case I might sue him (aforementioned trial lawyer and malpractice snouts), he sends me for some lab work (snout), and the results go to medical records (snout), then on to billing (snout) and to someone who writes me a letter with the results (snout). It contains some pamphlets on healthy living (snout) and a customer service response card (snout) so the clinic director can know if I am happy.

The bill for the lab work is sent (snout) to my claims processor (snout), who runs it by their fraud detectors (snout) and then checks the discount (snout) and in-network status (snout). If the claim is denied, then we repeat this loop several times (snoutis pluralis) until all the coding and paperwork is just so.

Then it goes to their payable department (snout), and they send a check to the receivable clerk (snout) at the clinic, and they send me a statement (snout) showing my bill was partially paid. My claims processor also produces an explanation of benefits (snout) that I can't understand, and mails it (snout) to me. Once in a while, they send me a card (snout) to see if I'm happy. Ecstatic; thanks for asking.

The claims processor then sends a bill (snout) to my Flex benefits administrator (snout) for the amount of the co-pay that my claims processor doesn't pay. The Flex people check my

TOOTH FAIRY GOVERNMENT

balance (snout) and send me a check (snout). The clinic sends me another bill (snout) for the balance and I send them a check. They process that check (snout) and send me a statement (snout) that the bill is paid.

Are you still with me? Our snout count is up to 26 if the claim goes through perfectly on the first pass, which doesn't happen very often anymore. But remember, that is just for the lab work I didn't need in the first place. Now we have to process the original office visit bill. No comment cards or healthy newsletter, so we only need to add 21 snouts; that puts us to 47. But wait, there's more.

We are self-insured at my company, so there is no obscene profit of an insurance company to factor in to our snout count. But we do have a benefits specialist (snout), a health coach (snout), and people in HR (snout) who help me straighten out my wrongly denied claims. And we pay consultants (snout) who pay other consultants (snout) to advise us on how to set all this up in compliance with the government's (that is a whole new trough) regulations for self-insured plans.

And then of course we have accountants (snout) who count our health care beans, and a law firm on retainer (snout) to help us stay in compliance with the government (I already did them) regulators and HEPA law. Bear in mind that those other firms with a snout in the trough also had their own accountants and lawyers and consultants and IT guys that could be added into the count - but that would be piling on.

And all of those snouts have to go to diversity training, and some pay union dues, and they go off to conferences where they learn the latest snout stuff, and if they work for the government they have too many holidays, vacation days, personal days, sick days, and work-at-home (yeah,, sure) days to keep track of. So they are out there just a-snorting and a-grunting and shaking the flies off their fat muddy backs even when they are not processing my bill.

By my count, that's 54 snouts in the trough, not including the government snout factory that regulates all and mandates half of this insanity. God forbid an MD and a Ph.D. could manage to exchange $15 on our own; no, we need 54 cubicle jockeys a-heppin' us to get it wrong.

And that, my friends, is what is wrong with health care. That is *all* that is wrong with health care.

That is how you turn a simple $15 exchange that any two crack-heads can accomplish unaided into a $175 cluster-grunt that takes 54 people with college degrees 6 months to get completed. And we make fun of crack-heads?

How about that public option/single payer idea? That just replaces my claims processor's private sector snouts with government snouts. And if you think the GS-8 at HHS oinks more efficiently than the Anthem contractors over there in Bangalore, then you are probably one of those crack-heads I have newfound respect for. Plus they retire at 50, so we have to count double to pay for the pensioners.

Are they fixing *any* of this up there in Congress? Nope. Those guys are just vibrating in place trying to finagle a way to stick that $175 bill to somebody that doesn't vote. When they are all done, it will be $350 and my grandkids will pay. There is not one snout coming out in any version of any Congressional reform bill.

These guys are all out of their minds. They had their chance this year to enact real health care reform; we get *our* chance again next November.

Smart People

If I wanted to research the Tea Party, I would not send Katie Couric to interview Sheryl Crow for Glamour magazine. But then again, it would not occur to me to ask for Shakira's advice on immigration law.

Prompted by Ms. Couric, Ms. Crow recently informed Glamour readers that all Tea Partiers are uneducated, angry, and ignorant. She forgot to say racist and violent - perhaps she should have wrote a list on her palm.

In March, I spoke at an event that the media described as a Tea Party, so I guess that makes me a Tea Partier. There were over a dozen speakers, all of us university educated, most with graduate degrees and several with doctorates. Granted, our degrees are only in economics, law, medicine, and commerce, not something rigorous like, say, music appreciation.

And besides, those really, really, *really* smart people in Washington who sneer with contempt for us common folk haven't got anything to brag about.

Those really smart people spent $700 billion on a stimulus plan that didn't stimulate. Every firm they took over to avoid bankruptcy went bankrupt. They gave $750 billion to banks that didn't need it. They bought Freddie and Fannie to stop them from bleeding millions every month; now they bleed billions.

Those really smart people played nice with North Korea, and Li'l Kim sank a South Korean destroyer. They put the sanction beatdown on Iran, I'm-a-bad-Jihad told them to go pound enriched uranium. They sent a retired smart guy to fix the Israeli/Palestinian conflict once and for all, and he managed to get Turkey caught up in it. Their hand-picked commander mutinied on them in Afghanistan.

Mexican drug lords invade Arizona and those really smart people put up a sign. Millions of barrels of oil invade the Gulf beaches and they count life jackets. Their anti-terrorist plan is apparently to hope that bad guys continue to blow duds while they dither around on Gitmo.

Those really smart people have Cabinet Secretaries ordering Under Secretaries to tell Deputy Secretaries to fetch coffee for Czars. They have commissions that study committee reports on task force recommendations. Their Senators don't ask, and their Supreme Court nominees don't tell. They boycott states they can't find on a map.

The Smartest One went personally to get us the Olympics and got stiffed. He went to get us Climate Change and got stiffed. He went to the G20 twice to get them to spend as much borrowed money as he does and he got stiffed both times. The President of the European Central Bank recently called the smart people's economic philosophy "incorrect", and the head of the European Union said our fiscal policies have put us on "the road to hell".

Just how bad do you have to be at running a government for the Europeans to think you suck at it? When Cash-4-Kias is your *best* stuff, even the Greeks laugh.

All those really smart people spent a whole year on a health care bill that none of them read and none of us wanted; now they find a two-scoop smart guy – Harvard professor *and* head of a think tank – to run it. He says he doesn't believe in market forces; he says he only trusts "leaders with plans".

Note to Dr. Berwick: every bankrupted CEO is a leader with a plan; every defeated general is a leader with a plan; every tin horn dictator is a leader with a plan; Jimmy Carter was a leader with a plan; the Detroit Lions have a leader with a plan. Market forces eat leaders with plans for lunch, as you are about to discover. Buckle up.

We tried all this stuff before. In May of 1939, President Roosevelt's Treasury Secretary Henry Morganthau – had this to say about the New Deal our modern day smart people revere: "We have tried spending money. We are spending more than we have ever spent before and it does not work.....We have never made good on our promises ... I say after eight years of this Administration we have just as much unemployment as when we started, and an enormous debt to boot".

The Liberty movement is not complicated: the socialists are ruining our country, and we are trying to stop them before they finish the job. You don't need a Ph.D. from Georgetown to pick a side; you need only to decide whether their theories are worth your liberty.

Well, are they?

Curing Cancer

If you were told you have cancer, would you ask Congress to: a) eliminate taxes on companies developing a cure, or b) eliminate their profits?

That strips the great debate right down to the nubs, now, doesn't it? Are you a free market capitalist or a state socialist?

Choose now, because once you are diagnosed with a potentially fatal disease it will be way too late to change your mind. As for me, I'm betting on Team Profit.

Because the sure cure for cancer is not going to be *discovered*; it does not exist. It must be *created* through someone's hard work; and it will be the rightful property of those people who develop it. They, not society, will own it.

The opportunity to profit from what you own is what makes people work harder, smarter, and most importantly when it comes to cancer cures, *faster*. Taxing those profits diminish the incentives to work hard, smart, and fast.

In a free market, whoever gets there first with the sure cure for cancer will become wealthy beyond comprehension – and well-earned would be an understatement. But when that happens, the state socialists will start whining about the income gap.

So here is question two - are you better off with: a) an income gap and your cancer cured, or b) pay equity and early death? Welcome, defectors from Team Tax.

Now at first, only rich people will be able to afford the sure cure for cancer. It will be just like cell phones and microwaves and hip replacements, where rich people will use their money and influence to be first in line.

At that point, the state socialists will be going berserk - outraged that only the rich are getting cured while the poor continue to die. They will demand that we tax the rich to even the playing field, and put a new "windfall profit" tax on the cancer cure providers.

If the world were a caring contest, that would be a good idea; but the world is a paying contest, so it's a stupid one.

The high profits from selling the first units of the cure to the rich provide the investment capital needed to expand production and lower unit costs, making the cure for cancer available to less-wealthy people. If you tax those profits, there is no money to reinvest and the cure will be only for the rich forever.

Question three - how do you get more money out of rich people: a) giving them a cure for their cancer in return, or b) increasing their marginal tax rate? Team Tax is mow losing members faster than John Wayne Bobbitt.

The profit/investment/cost reduction cycle repeats and accelerates, so very soon the sure cure for cancer will be accessible to even the poorest members of our society. The fun will really begin when Walmart starts selling it – poor people will be doing cartwheels into the stores, while the millionaire talking heads on MSNBC will still be whining about the greeters not getting benefits.

Risk and reward, profit and loss, producing things people want at prices they can afford – this is how free market capitalism works; more importantly *why* capitalism works.

Profits, not taxes, will bring the sure cure for cancer to the whole of society, along with all the other products and services that improve living standards for everyone. If we want to raise living standards, it is foolish to tax profits.

If you Team Tax people would rather see people die than see someone make more money than you, then please do not lecture me about morality. If you hate profits, then you hate poor people, and it's about time somebody called you out.

In our tax-and-grant, government-run medical research industry, the only guys making a profit are the folks selling those lapel ribbons we have been wearing for the past 30 years for all the diseases that the all the non-profits haven't cured yet.

Personally, I would rather cure a disease than show how much I care by wearing a ribbon. That is why I am a free market capitalist; that is why I am a Libertarian. That's why you should be, too. Now, before you contract a fatal disease.

Card Check Cannibals

Like many people, I oppose unions on principle. That principle is: never negotiate the dinner menu with cannibals.

American workers overwhelmingly reject unionism. According to a 2010 study by university researchers Barry Hirsch and David Macpherson, only 7.2% of private sector workers belonged to unions in 2009. 93% prefer to work union-free.

Union apologists blame their declining numbers on threats and intimidation of workers by evil capitalist employers. Nice try, Norma Rae, but only 32.7% of *public* sector workers choose to be unionized, and last time I checked, John Galt was not running the Department of Labor.

As a guy who came up from the factory floor, I can assure you that workers are not stupid, gullible, or easily intimidated. 90% of private sector workers and 70% of public employees know they have a right to organize a union, and have freely chosen not to.

But union bosses, like socialists everywhere, do not recognize the will of the people; they claim to *embody* the will of the people. So they have tasked their wholly owned subsidiary, the Democrat Party, with depriving workers of their right to vote on workplace representation - to replace the secret ballot election with imposition of a union by the State. This is an idea so hideous that even George McGovern – hardly a capitalist tool - came out of retirement to oppose it.

The Senate Bill eliminating union elections is cynically titled the "Employee Free Choice Act", commonly referred to as Card Check. If Congress were subject to truth in advertising laws, it would be titled "Employee No Choice Act", as its sole purpose is to deprive workers the right to choose.

If enacted, Card Check will empower the government to impose a union on any employer when 50% of employees sign interest cards. It also authorizes the government to impose contract terms if the union does not accept a company offer within 90 days. It does not take a rocket surgeon to figure out that there is no incentive for either party to bargain, so the practical impact of the Bill is for government to set labor prices and benefits. That should work well.

TOOTH FAIRY GOVERNMENT

Now, when it was Al Gore's job on the line, Democrats were the party of no-chad-left-behind, remember? Every single vote was precious, even the ones that weren't cast. No such luck for us working stiffs; we are just an untapped source of union dues which funnel back into the Dems campaign coffers – a herd of cows to be milked each payday.

State-imposed unionism is the antithesis of libertarian individualism in the workplace; economic subjugation and economic sovereignty are diametrically opposite ideals. But opposition to unions is justified on practical grounds.

Unions protect incompetents from the consequences of their own actions, and force those consequences onto others – observe the Milwaukee Public Schools and General Motors. Individualism breeds exceptionalism, and exceptionalism is intolerable to the union collectivist.

Over my career I have been involved in five union organizing campaigns at three firms; each one was marked by unions inflicting physical violence to persons and property to coerce the signing of interest cards. Unions targeted the most vulnerable to get the number needed to call an election. The idea that NLRB rules disadvantage unions is laughable.

The unions were defeated overwhelmingly in each one of those elections, and four of the five campaigns occurred during Democrat administrations, so the "stacked NLRB deck" argument won't fly. People who signed interest cards under duress voted against the unions in the secret ballot. That is the problem Card Check solves for the unions.

Under Card Check, unions would have been imposed upon those workers by their own government without any election. Pause for a moment to reflect on the obscenity of that proposition: the right to remain union-free will be denied by the very government tasked with protecting that right.

The Hirsch and Macpherson study also listed the unionization rate among public workers by state. It is no coincidence that the 10 states which are more than 50% unionized are the 10 states teetering on insolvency – Wisconsin among them.

We can now add government and education to the list of American industries devoured by the union cannibals: mining, shipbuilding, logging, steel, automobiles, appliances, electronics, textiles, airlines, machine tools, consumer products, furniture, musical instruments – the list is too long to recite.

To a cannibal, success is being the last one in his tribe to die of starvation. His union campaign is your invitation to dinner; Card Check lets the government RSVP on your behalf. Fight back now, before it is too late.

Jobs

None of us who actually create jobs were surprised at the dismal May employment numbers, while the President's economists were shocked. What does that tell you?

Excluding temporary census workers, only 25,000 private sector jobs were added in May, less than 20% of the number needed just to keep pace with the growth in the workforce. The President's crack team of Keynesian number crunchers had forecasted around 500,000.

Mr. Obama somehow managed to blame businesses for the blown call, chiding them for unwarranted hiring reticence in the face of an expanding GDP. In doing so, he displayed an unnerving lack of understanding of how jobs are created and how GDP is aggregated.

Businesses do not hire workers to grow the economy, to make a President's economic recovery plan work, or to keep some magic ratio to GDP; we only hire workers to meet increased demand for our products and services. And demand is not growing, it is shrinking.

Government is "stimulating" the economy with deficit spending that exceeds 9% of GDP, yet total GDP growth drops to around 3% when consumer spending and business investment are added. You do the math.

While the government continues to insist that its stimulus schemes have jump-started the economy into recovery, the evidence says otherwise. Common sense would tell you that giving California teachers a raise will not stimulate an Ohio foundry to recall its laid off pipefitters.

And who in their right mind would re-open a closed foundry or build a new one, facing increased taxes on profits and capital gains, a hostile regulatory environment, new and uncertain health care obligations, VAT, cap and trade energy rationing, and union card check?

Nobody would, nobody is, and nobody will. And that, Mr. President, is why those Ohio pipefitters are never getting their jobs back – ever.

This is the cruel reality that government economists haven't programmed into their computers' forecasting models. History is not repeating itself because humans act rationally and circumstances have changed.

Why should an entrepreneur risk his depleted 401(k) to start a business that must pay higher minimum wages, provide mandated benefits, and comply with new health care record-keeping requirements, just so he can pay higher taxes on any profits that might remain? Why not take a six figure government job and be set for life?

We know how to create jobs; 40 million new American jobs were created in the last quarter of the 20th century, the era of deregulation, tax reduction, fiscal restraint, monetary moderation, and free markets.

And we know how to kill jobs; 8 million jobs have been lost in the past three years, the new era of increased regulation, tax increases, fiscal irresponsibility, monetary expansion, and government interventions into markets.

The key to economic recovery is not mysterious; we need only to extract the government monkey wrench and the market machinery will turn again on its own.

Eliminate taxes on business earnings, capital gains, and inheritance; de-regulate over-regulated industries; dismantle corporate welfare subsidies, repeal health care, and stabilize the currency; stop cap and trade, stop card check, and vote down any new legislation that has the words "comprehensive" or "reform" in its title.

When markets work, people do. Until the administration economists grasp that concept, they will continue to be shocked that their predictions don't come true.

TOOTH FAIRY GOVERNMENT

Thou Shall Not Steal

There are only two ways to get the money to pay for government: either tax Americans who are living, or steal it from generations of Americans not born yet.

Deficit spending is stealing from future generations; in the fiscal year coming to a close this month, we have stolen nearly $2 trillion more of their money, and Congress will take another heaping helping when they pass the 2010 appropriations bills in the upcoming weeks.

You don't need a Ph.D. in economics to grasp the issue here: it is wrong to steal money from your kids.

If you don't get that, you might as well stop reading now and go knock off a liquor store or beat up a homeless person or whatever it is you do for recreation. I won't be able to fix you; maybe my Pastor Paula could take a crack at it.

This year, we will only pay for 58% of what government spends; we will borrow the rest, leaving it to future generations to repay the debt. Are you ok with stealing $5,400 from your grandkids and their grandkids? That is your per capita share of the deficit this year – the amount of spending you did not pay for. No different than driving away from the pump, or skating out on the waitress.

To pay for the government we have, each one of us would have to take a 70% hike in every single one of the taxes we pay. Is anyone willing to do that? If not, then the ethical thing to do would be to cut government spending down to what we *are* willing to pay for ourselves – to cut it almost in half. It is not as difficult as we might think, but the "how to" is another post for another day.

We could have (and should have) an honest political debate over how much to tax ourselves and what to spend that money on. People of good will can disagree over the proper scope and role of government in a free society. But we don't have honest debates anymore; we have mindless shouting matches where each side calls the other side evil for thinking differently, and they both tell you someone else will pay for the promises they make to get your vote.

The one lie that *is* evil is the lie of the free lunch; it doesn't matter whether it is democrat or republican baloney between the bread. There is no such a thing; we are stealing our kid's lunch money to buy happy meals for ourselves. That is morally reprehensible – it is shameful when Republicans do it, and it is shameful when Democrats do it, and it is shameful when we let them both do it.

The Congressional Budget Office estimates it will take 100 years to pay it back the $24 trillion of debt we will have accumulated by 2019, just 10 years from now. I will be retiring about then, but you young people will still have a lifetime of paying to look forward to, and so will your heirs. Your share will run into the hundreds of thousands of dollars. Most of your taxes will go to pay interest on the debt. This is what happens when you don't vote.

Oblivious to the fact that we can't afford half of the government we have now, the socialists want to impose even *more* government. It is still a free country, sort of; if they do not think they are being taxed enough, they can write a check to the IRS and pay more. That would be the honorable thing, and I would admire them for it.

But they won't – they insist on putting *your* money where *their* mouth is.

We are tired of other people telling us what to do, what to say, and what to think. We don't need government's permission to live our lives. We have had it with moralizing hypocrites – of both parties - using the power of the state to shove their beliefs down our throats.

Government is not our master; it is our servant, our Cabana Boy. The Cabana Boy doesn't tell us what to do. The Cabana boy picks up the cigarette butts; he doesn't tell us we can't smoke on our own private property. So shut up and go fix a bridge, Cabana Boy – and quit stealing my grandchildren's money.

Congress is supposed to represent, not to rule; and most certainly not to steal. We need to elect Representatives who understand that. Tammy Baldwin doesn't.

Liberty is the absence of government in choice. Tyranny is the absence of choice in government. Choose Liberty. Choose Tim, Not Tammy.

The 100 Yard Dash

Among liberal circles the principle of outcome equality has largely displaced the notion of opportunity equality as a barometer of social justice.

While some conservatives have criticized the mechanisms by which the goal of outcome equality is pursued, few have been willing to directly challenge the ideal of outcome equality itself.

This is unfortunate, because the notion of outcome equality deserves to be challenged; the pursuit of outcome equality diminishes opportunity equality, and it destroys competition.

And yet, so blurred have these two notions become that inequality of outcome is often accepted as evidence of inequality of opportunity. For example, advocates for pay equity point to income disparity (outcome inequality) between genders as de facto evidence of unfair discrimination (opportunity inequality) in pay systems.

This idea is *exactly* wrong. If opportunity is equal, outcomes will always be unequal; conversely equal outcome is only possible when opportunity is forced to be unequal. The principle is easily illustrated in the example of the 100 yard dash.

If 50 people run a 100 yard dash under one set of rules, there will be 50 different outcomes. No two will finish exactly together, because no two individuals are alike in potential. The only way to have all 50 people finish together is to apply different rules for the slower runners than are applied to the faster ones.

Since the slow cannot be coerced to run any faster, the *only possible* means to achieve outcome equality is force the faster runners to run slower, or run longer, or start later. Creating equal outcomes can only be achieved by preventing the most able from reaching their full potential.

This principle is universal – regardless the type of human endeavor, outcome equality can only be achieved through coercive restriction of the most able. That is the first reason outcome equality is a bad idea. It makes the most able less able.

TOOTH FAIRY GOVERNMENT

The second reason it is a bad idea is that is makes the least able less able, too. Unequal opportunity diminishes competition, and competition is a wonderful thing, as can also be illustrated in the example of the 100 yard dash.

For the slow runners to improve their lot, they will train and work to run faster and be rewarded by moving up the order of finish. The fast runners will react to this threat to their positions by training harder and running faster, too.

Competition makes *both* the good runners and bad runners better. While there is a disparity in outcome – everyone is running faster. This is the inevitable result of opportunity equality.

However, if the rules are rigged to insure equality of outcome -- i.e. everyone finishes together regardless of ability -- there is no incentive for *anyone* to run faster, or to maintain their current speed. The absence of competition makes the both the good runners and bad runners worse.

The principles illustrated in the example of the 100 yard dash govern every aspect of our lives, and we ignore them at our peril. Abandoning the ideal of equal opportunity to pursue the ideal of equal outcome is making us a society of slow runners.

Our public school systems fully embrace the ideal of equality of outcome, from wage fixing for teachers to the attempts to eliminate grades for students. The result over the past 30 years is an alarming decline from among the top countries in the world in student performance to out of the top 15 and falling. Everyone is running slower.

Contrast education to telecommunications over the same 30 years. Since deregulation, market competition has brought us technologies unimaginable at that time. To be sure Bill Gates has become wealthy beyond the average Joe's comprehension. But even the below-average Joes have cell phones, computers, and 2 cents a minute long distance to anywhere in the world. Everyone is running faster.

The trajectories of education and telecommunications are not accidental. They are the inevitable results of two distinctly different ideals of equality put into practice in the real world. In North and South Korea we can see that the same divergent trajectories occur when whole societies choose outcome equality over opportunity equality.

The United States Declaration of Independence properly enumerates self-evident and unalienable rights endowed to each individual person by our Creator.

It does not suggest that He really meant for us to be entitled by reason of age, class, race, gender, religion, or membership. It does not reveal a right to an equal slice of the happiness pie, apportioned by government according to the whims of contemporary political fad. Rights, like potential, are an individual thing.

Those who hold up equality of outcome as a barometer of social justice are entirely wrong. Those who advocate for it are deeply misguided.

The public good is only served when each of us runs our own 100 yard dash just as fast as we possibly can.

Compassion

The dividing line between compassion and tyranny has a name: it is called *coercion*. It is the border that encircles libertarian geography on the political map.

Few would argue with our bedrock libertarian principle: it is unjust to initiate force or fraud against another person. Don't you agree?

And yet we force people to join unions, force people to pay arbitrary prices for goods, services, and labor, force people to purchase insurance, force people to fund activities and organizations and activities they find immoral, force people to give up their property, force people to surrender their income, force people to lend money to others, force people to attend a particular school.

We do all this (and more) in the name of compassion; that is a distortion of the term's meaning. Compassion is when 95% of us tend to the truly needy 5% on our own volition; tyranny is forcing 5% to provide unearned benefits to the 95%.

Compassion is giving poor parents the same school choice that rich parents have; tyranny is forcing Milwaukee kids to attend public schools where only 6% will be taught to read proficiently and painters make over $100,000.

60% of Americans now get more income *from* government than they give *to* it; that number will raise to over 70% when the new health care bill kicks in. This is not a safety net; it is an ATM where 3 of us deposit and 7 withdraw.

We use State force to compel, and we also use State force to prohibit: from eating certain foods, engaging in certain behaviors, traveling to certain places, buying certain products, engaging in certain forms of commerce - the list is too numerous to recite. We have *eight times* the incarceration rate of other developed countries - such is our preoccupation with enacting prohibitions and punishing each other.

Tearing families apart over victimless crimes is not compassionate. And if society itself can be a victim, then why is adultery not a class A felony? Can you think of anything which has destroyed more families, plunged more people into poverty, or inflicted more emotional trauma?

Libertarians believe that all voluntary exchange is just, and that any initiation of coercive force is unjust. That is where we part company with liberals on the social issues, often drawing criticism for a presumed lack of compassion.

The dividing line is clear: I have a right to form a union; no right to force you to join it. I have a right to health care; no right to force you to buy it for me. I have a right to choose my own lifestyle; no right to force you to subsidize it.

Liberals would never think of stealing your money themselves; but they have no qualms about employing the State to do the job. I doubt they would break into your house and snoop through your private files and records, but they set the State onto that task regularly.

If you employ a person to initiate force on your behalf, your prison sentence will be called *justice* and you will be called an *accomplice*. But if you employ the State to employ a person to initiate force on your behalf, then it will be called *social justice* and you will be called a *progressive*.

Libertarians prefer to use terms for their intended meanings. We do not consider initiation of force to be progress; we do not consider deprivation of liberty to be justice.

Liberals mistake and even misrepresent any libertarian objections to the *means* of achieving a goal as disagreement with the goal itself – Rand Paul is the latest victim of the grindhouse. The lesson to be learned is that a Constitutionalist should not engage in debate with a Frivolist.

Besides, the CRA makes the libertarian's case, not the liberal's. Half a century of State coercion has not cured racial disparity, just as State coercion has not eliminated income disparity, poverty, crime, violence, corruption, or drug use, and has not improved educational performance, economic competitiveness, domestic security, or a whole list of things that matter to all of us.

The things that we all value most - health, prosperity, opportunity, family, friends, love, happiness, freedom, pride, accomplishment, career, beauty, education, faith, security, material abundance, creative expression, community – are not things that can be compelled to materialize, and they are non-transferable.

Each of us defines them for ourselves, attains them individually, and decides for ourselves when we have accumulated enough of them. They can not be given to you by the coercive power of the State; they can only be taken.

That is why the line between compassion and tyranny must be drawn with a sharp pen; and why it must never be crossed.

Equality

Equality of opportunity is a buffet. Equality of outcome is prison food. We are a buffet nation; we hate prison food.

There is nothing more that needs to be said.

ABOUT THE AUTHOR

Tim Nerenz is a business executive with 35 years of experience in manufacturing, mining, national security, and energy.

He holds three graduate degrees in business, an AGDM and MBA from Athabasca University in Alberta, Canada, and a Ph.D. in Business Administration from Northcentral University in Arizona.

When he is not working, writing, or speaking, Tim spends his time with his wife of 26 years, Joanne. Tim and Joanne split their time between Wisconsin and Florida.

His weekly blog "Dr. Tim's Moment of Clarity" can be found on the Facebook Group page of the same name, or on his website www.timnerenz.com.